E-Z READER:

LEARNING TO READ THE PHONICS WAY

A READING PRIMER
FOR THE ADULT NON-READER

by

PERFECTO G. QUERUBIN, JR.

Consultant
Sharon Yates, M.Ed., Ed.D
Rio Grande University
Rio Grande, Ohio

Illustrators
Annabel Amores Walsh
and Maggie Suson

dp
DISTINCTIVE PUBLISHING CORP.

E-Z Reader: Learning to Read the Phonics Way
By Perfecto G. Querubin, Jr.
Copyright 1993 by Perfecto G. Querubin, Jr.

Consultant: Sharon Yates, M.Ed., Ed.D.
Illustrators: Annabel Amores Walsh and Maggie Suson

Published by Distinctive Publishing Corp.
P. O. Box 17868
Plantation, Florida 33318-7868
Printed in the United States of America

ISBN: 0-942963-34-2
Library of Congress No.: 93-15850
Price: $14.95

Library of Congress Cataloging-in-Publication Data

Querubin, Perfecto G., 1940-
    E-Z Reader : learning to read the phonics way: a reading primer for the adult non-reader / by Perfecto G. Querubin, Jr.;
consultant, Sharon Yates; illustrators, Annabel Amores Walsh and Maggie Suson.
        p. cm.
    Includes bibliographical references (p.).
    ISBN 0-942963-34-2 : $14.95
    1. Reading (adult education)—United States. 2. Reading (elementary)—United States—Phonetic method. 3. Adult learning—
United States. I. Yates, Sharon. II. Title.   III. Title: EZ reader.
LC5225.R4Q47   1993
428.4'071'5—dc20   93-15850
                                                                        CIP

ACKNOWLEDGMENTS

I should like to express my profound gratitude to Hedy Franco and Sharon Yates. Hedy — who received her Master's Degree in Education at the University of West Virginia — initially thought of designing this primer for the adult non-reader and contributed useful ideas in the presentation of materials. Sharon — who earned her Doctorate Degree in Education Administration at the same institution — has been teaching reading education at the University of Rio Grande for fourteen years. She patiently went through several revisions of this primer, posing questions, giving advice, offering her insights and criticism. I offer special thanks to my wife, Lela, for her encouragement and abiding faith that this primer will help someone.

If one individual profits by this primer, the expectation will be justified and the effort richly rewarded.

TABLE OF CONTENTS

INSTRUCTION MANUAL

FOR WHOM AND WHY THIS BOOK WAS WRITTEN

My idea for a reading primer dates back over a decade, when my eldest child, Patrick, now seventeen years of age, had mastered the alphabet. I then taught him the way I had learned how to read. I introduced him to the *Cartilla*. In Spanish, it literally means small letters. It also means a primer. The *Cartilla* is a set of consonant-vowel combinations beginning with ba, be, bi, bo, bu, which I memorized when I was in grade one as part of my initial reading program. Knowing how tedious it was to learn by rote, I tried to make it easier for Patrick to recognize the consonant-vowel combinations and keywords by pasting pictures and illustrations next to the words. He learned to read before he began grade one. I taught his sister Linne and his brother Perry the same way. They also learned to read before they started grade one.

I discussed the possibility of preparing a phonetic reading primer with my brother-in-law, who is a commercial artist. He did some illustrations, then abandoned the idea. Perhaps he made the illustrations, not out of conviction, but to humor me. If either of us had had more conviction, the project might have been finished long ago. Years later, I would meet individuals who shared the idea that a reading primer based on blending or fusing consonants and vowels is feasible.

In 1984, our family came to the United States. More by accident than by design, two more children were added to the family: Peter, now seven, and Lizl, now five. Peter, like most boys of his age, went to preschool. One day in April 1989, he came home and announced that he knew his alphabet. That was nothing to be excited about. Any normal child of his age, when exposed to the alphabet, learns to recognize the letters. It occurred to me, though, that it was a good time to teach him how to read. I taught him the way I had taught his brothers and older sister. He learned to read before he was in kindergarten.

Lizl is now in kindergarten. She learned to read the same way. In her class, she is the only one who can read. She does not just read beginner reading books of the "I am Mike" type. She reads children's classics, including Cinderella, Hansel and Gretel, and Ariel, the Little Mermaid books.

I showed this "primitive" reading primer to Ms. Hedy Franco and Sharon Yates in May, 1989. Hedy was then earning her master's degree in Education; Sharon was completing her doctorate in Education Administration at the College of Graduate Studies at The University of West Virginia. (Both earned their degrees that year.) At that time, the problem of adult illiteracy was prominent in the public mind. Like a magnet, the problem drew our attention. I researched phonics as an initial reading system and its possible use by adult non-readers. Sharon suggested two books which would serve me well as starting points: Professor Jeanne S. Chall's *Learning to Read: The Great Debate* (1967) and Rudolph Flesch's *Why Johnny Can't Read and What You Can Do About It* (1955). These two books convinced me that not only is a phonics method based on blending consonants and vowels feasible, there is an actual need for it.

Rudolph Flesch, writing on the efficiency of a phonic approach to beginning reading, says:

In a language with a perfect phonetic alphabet, this is a very short and simple process. Dr. Frank Laubach, famous for his work in teaching half the world to read and write, always starts by working out a phonetic alphabet for the language with which he is dealing; he then teaches the natives, in very short order, how to read and write. For instance in his book, *Teaching the World to Read*, he writes of the application of the method to the most widely spoken dialect of the Philippines. "*It is easy*," he writes, "*for a man with average intelligence to read in one day using these lessons. Many of the people have learned to read in two hours, some even in one hour.*"

Yes, if you have a language with a perfectly phonetic alphabet, you are in a sort of dream world where teaching to read and write is no problem (pp. 22-23, italics supplied).

On the other hand, those who had extensive experience with disabled readers, like Fernald, Orton, and Monroe, have demonstrated that phonics is an effective remedial measure even for severe reading disabilities (Chall, *op. cit.*, pp. 170-171, 176-177).

It is not correct to say that because the phonic method worked well for me and my children, it should do well for others — especially, adult non-readers. What can be said is that it works for some people.

Not everyone is comfortable with the whole-word method of learning how to read. A tour of the primary school system shows that some children have difficulty learning to read under the whole-word method. Some who start well with it eventually develop reading difficulties. According to A. J. Harris, "...no new approach has been able to lessen significantly the proportion of children who make disappointing progress in beginning reading" (*How to Increase Reading Ability*, 5th ed., A. J. Harris, 1970, p. 79). This means that every year we add to the number of children with reading difficulties. These children are on the way to becoming "functional illiterates" or worse, plain illiterates.

What all this underscores is that there may not be a single effective method of teaching beginners how to read, whether they are children or adults. There is a need for an alternative or supplementary method for those who cannot cope well with the whole-word method. This primer could fit into that role.

This system is basically a phonetic-syllabic approach to learning how to read. It is designed primarily for the adult non-reader, bilingual Americans having difficulty reading English, and others who may be having difficulty with the whole-word method of learning how to read.

I understand that many adult non-readers are constrained to use primary school materials in learning how to read because there is a dearth of materials for their use. This is not an auspicious beginning. It is unfortunate. "...W. S. Gray found that adults learned to read efficiently when the materials were functional and suited to their mature interests" ("Reading," p. 10, in Vol. 19, *Encyclopedia Britannica*, 1973). Even children are challenged more by words that are appropriate to their level of intelligence rather than their reading skill level (Chall, *op. cit.*, p. 171). Further, the adult non-reader's self-esteem — already low, we can imagine — will suffer yet another blow. Though an adult non-reader and a child in elementary school are on the same plane, reading-wise, they are psychologically worlds apart. Using the same materials for both may be counter-productive for the former. Citing Knowles, J.R. Kidd (1976) points to an important difference between a child and an adult.

A child first sees himself as a completely dependent personality. He sees himself in his first consciousness as a being completely dependent upon the adult world to make decisions for him. ...But at some point he starts experiencing the joy of deciding things for himself... To be an adult means to be self-directing. Now at the point at which this change occurs, *there develops in the human being a deep psychological need to be perceived by himself and by others as being indeed self-directing.* This is the concept that lies at the heart of andragogy.

Andragogy is based upon the insight that *the deepest need of an adult is to be treated as an adult, to be treated as a self-directing person, to be treated with respect...* (*How Adults Learn*, p. 36, italics supplied).

Hence, this primer.

THE THEORETICAL, EXPERIMENTAL AND RESEARCH BASES OF PRESENT TEACHING PRACTICES

I am aware of the controversy surrounding how best to teach beginning reading. Dr. Rudolph Flesch is quite emphatic in his advocacy of phonics, not as the best, but as the only approach to learning how to read. Citing studies and experiments over the years, he claims that the look-and-say method (another name for whole-word method) used in most schools is the cause of reading failure (*Why Johnny Can't Read*, R. Flesch 1955; *Why Johnny Still Can't Read*, R. Flesch, 1980). Equally stringent in his criticism of the whole-word approach to initial reading is Samuel Blumenfeld. To him, the whole-word method is based "...on two great confusions: the first, that learning how to read is the same as learning the language; the second, that learning how to read is the same process as reading." He concludes: "...no child actually learns how to read our written language in that way (whole-word method), and our colleges are full of the new illiterates to prove it" (*The New Illiterates*, S. Blumenfeld, 1973, pp. 212-213).

According to Harris, the most common criticism against basal readers utilizing the whole-word method is that they are artificial, stilted, monotonous, unduly repetitious and have a very limited vocabulary (*How to Increase Reading Ability*, 5th ed., A. Harris, 1970, p. 65).

On the other hand, it is claimed that phonics reduces reading to a number of mechanical procedures which produced individuals adept at working their way through a word; that kind of reading became equated with "facility in calling words" (*Principles and Practices of Teaching Reading*, 6th ed., Heilman, Blair and Rupley, 1986, pp. 132-133). However, it does not give enough attention to the thought provoking side of reading (Harris, *op. cit.*, p. 62), and is thus regarded as the natural enemy of reading for meaning (Heilman, *et al.*, *op. cit.*, p. 136).

A middle-of-the-ground view is expressed by Dr. Harry Forgan who claims that both methods are necessary:

> Regardless of which approach is taken to initial reading instruction, there are some words that your child must learn by sight. As mentioned, approximately 85 percent of the words in the English language follow the principles of phonics. There are some words and some parts of words which must be memorized because they do not follow phonics. *The old argument of the phonic method versus the sight word method is no longer an issue. Reading specialists and teachers realize that both are needed for successful reading* (*Help Your Child Learn to Read*, H. Forgan, 1975, pp. 63-64, italics supplied).

This is not an isolated view. "Rather than taking extreme positions for or against phonics instruction, teachers need to analyze how they will teach children to learn" (Heilman, *et. al.*, *op. cit.*, p. 137).

A similar thought is expressed by A. J. Harris:

> It is also noteworthy that no new approach has been able to lessen significantly the proportion of children who make disappointing progress in beginning reading. It may be that some of the children who fail with one approach might not have failed with another approach. Perhaps beginners with poor visual perception would do better with intensive phonics; those with poor auditory perception, with "look-and-say"; those with generally poor perception, with emphasis on reinforcement through tracing and writing. This, however, has not been demonstrated in research as [sic] yet.*Thus, balanced eclectic approach which uses visual, auditory, touch and kinesthetic cues in combination and develops word identification and comprehension simultaneously, seems safer and less likely to produce difficulties than any method which relies primarily on one sensory avenue or stresses one important side of reading while neglecting another* (Harris, op.cit., p. 79, italics supplied).

Barbara Johnson puts the matter this way:

> Since there is no one best approach to teaching children to read, experienced teachers currently use the best from each of several approaches. As a result, the teacher now has to be knowledgeable about a variety of reading approaches and materials. In a varied

reading program no single approach is used. LEA (Language Experience Approach), basal, and phonics are all taught. One approach may be emphasized over another due to an individual child's strengths and weaknesses (*Helping Your Child Achieve in School*, B. Johnson, 1st ed., 1985, p. 81).

I agree with this line of thought. Although this primer leans heavily toward the phonetic method and the linguistic approach advocated by Leonard Bloomfield, it deviates and adds to the latter when theory, research, and experimentation indicate a more efficient approach. The Bloomfield method, favored by Professor Chall as an initial reading method (*Learning to Read: The Great Debate*, 1967, p. 83), is summarized by Harris, (*op. cit.*, pp. 70-71) as follows:

1. start with teaching the identification of all alphabet letters by name (not sound);

2. begin with words in which each letter represents only one phonetic value;

3. use the principle of minimal variation, employing a list of words alike except for one letter, such as ban, Dan, can, fan, man, and the like;

4. do not teach rules about letter-sound correspondences; children will evolve correct responses when sound and spelling correspond in regular fashion; and

5. employ learned words in sentences, such as, "Nan can fan Dan."

This primer adopts the principle of minimal variation and keeps as close to it as possible. It employs the practice words in sentences. Outside of the sight words, which are introduced as part of the lessons, no other words are used in the exercise sentences. This is in keeping with the finding of Professor Chall that "[a] simplified phonic approach which uses words controlled for spelling regularity is more effective than a phonic emphasis that uses common, irregularly spelled words for practice" (Chall, *op. cit.*, p. 177). Though this observation was made in relation to remedial measures for disabled readers, there is no reason why it can not apply to an adult beginning reader, since the obvious purpose of the simplified approach is to prevent confusing the learner and facilitate learning.

This primer does not follow Bloomfield's prescription that sound values of the letters and rules on letter-sound correspondences should not be taught. Experiments by Winch (1925) with children and by Bishop (1964) with adults tend to show that direct teaching of the sound values of letters can improve word learning. In the Bishop experiment, about half of those receiving word training could not induce the letter-sound correspondences without direct instruction, although the adults involved had had considerable previous experience with alphabetic languages (Chall, *op. cit.*, pp. 116-117).

The primer goes further; it teaches the non-reader how to sound the letters in combination. There is good reason for doing so. Dr. Orton, who had extensive experience with disabled readers, believed that phonic training, to be valuable, must be followed by adequate practice in blending (or fusing) the separate sound values to form words (Chall, *op. cit.*, p. 177). This belief has since been justified. Experiments conducted subsequent to those of Winch and Bishop have categorically shown the beneficial effects of this practice.

After three years, in 1967, a similar experiment was conducted by Drs. W.E. Jeffrey and S. Jay Samuels, then at the University of California in Los Angeles. Instead of adults, Jeffrey and Samuels took 60 kindergartners from a public school, and instead of Arabic characters they used arbitrary, odd-shaped symbols. The children in the word group were taught four nonsense words — mo, so ba, be, and those in the letter group were taught the sounds of *s, m, a, e*. The words to be learned were *se, sa, me and ma*.

Jeffrey and Samuels' results were the same as Bishop's. The letter-trained group was clearly superior to the word-trained group. Ten years later, in 1977, Dr. Douglas Carnine of the University of Oregon conducted another similar experiment. He tried to make the situation as much as possible like a classroom situation. So he used regular English letters, gave the children more words and letters to learn, and added some irregular words to those to be learned. Carnine's results confirmed those of Bishop and Jeffrey and Samuels. Phonics-first won hands down over look-and-say. *Both the Jeffrey and Samuels experiment and Carnine' recapitulation had an important added feature — the letter-trained children were taught not only what sounds the letters stood for but also how to "blend" those sounds — saying* mmm, *and* ee, *and then blending them to say* me.

This special training in blending was based on the idea that learning tasks must be analyzed to find their component subskills. Then these subskills must be taught in a strict sequence — a hierarchy. A higher skill in such a sequence is taught only when the lower subskill has been fully mastered. Only this way can a complex skill be taught so that it can be performed without mistakes (*Why Johnny Still Can't Read*, R. Flesch, 1980, pp. 34-35, emphasis supplied).

Elsewhere, it has been shown that solving a problem becomes easier when the problem is broken up into two or more smaller and manageable problems (see *Thinking Better*, David Lewis & James Greene, 1982, p. 201-203; also *Brain Power*, Karl Albrecht, 1980, p. 185).

To a beginner, "reading" even a short two syllable word like "baby" can be an intimidating "problem," especially when the beginner is an adult. Showing him that the word can be separated into two syllables, "bay" and "bee," not only makes his job easier, it gives him an insight into what takes place when he decodes or "reads" a word.

Most letters are associated with one sound. Some, though, are associated with more than one sound. The letter C, for instance, sounds like K or S depending on what letter follows it. Emphasis on the rules applicable to such changes or the absence of change will help the learner in decoding new words and also in retaining and remembering words that have become part of his reading vocabulary. "Rules... must later become automatic, and finally, forgotten so as [sic] to prevent their interfering in the process of skillful decoding" (*Teaching About Phonics*, A. J. Mazurkiewicz, 1976, p. 105). "The discovery of a rule is easier than rote memory and the effect lasts longer" (Edmund B. Blair, *op. cit.*, 1988, pp. 109). "Deriving rules, no matter how absurd, is a useful memory system" (*Ibid*, p. 110).

The primer starts with the sounds that consonants make, then it introduces the learner to the long and short vowel sounds. To be able to associate the sounds with the particular letters, it is necessary to be thoroughly familiar with such letters. One author says that "It is actually *more desirable and easier* for a young child (and very likely an adult learner) *initially to learn whole words already familiar through oral language*, rather than learn abstract letters... There is no evidence that alphabet identification ought to be treated as the first skill in early literacy; it makes more sense for children to learn to identify letters after they have learned a number of sight words." (*Literacy Development in Early Years*, L.M. Morrow, 1989, p. 130, italics supplied). I think though, that such an approach is good only if you are adopting a method that relies on the whole-word method of teaching how to read. A phonetic approach will definitely require familiarity with the letters. At any rate, the primer introduces a few sight words at the beginning of each lesson to enable the construction of practice sentences. These sentences are just as important as the exercise words. Beginning readers retain and remember words better when they are used in a meaningful context. The learner will remember the exercise words even better if he uses them in his own sentences (see *Remembering and Forgetting*, Edmund B. Blair, 1988, pp. 70-71 and pp. 104-105). "The act of structuring information in itself aids understanding and learning" (D. Lewis and J. Greene, *op. cit.*, 1982, p. 179).

The first part of the primer does not extensively use words with silent letters, blends, digraphs, or words with vowel sounds other than the long or short sound, and it does not separate the dual phonetic values associated with some letters like c, g, q or s. In a series of experiments performed in 1963, Levin found that although at the beginning it takes longer to learn dual associations for letters (*e.g.*, to learn that g is pronounced as hard g in "go" and as soft g in "gem") than to learn one association at a time, dual association learning has a greater transfer value. Levin postulates that Bloomfield's approach of teaching single associations at a time may be easier at the beginning, but in the long run, its transfer value in reading irregularly-spelled words may be limited (Chall, *op. cit.*, p. 117).

One feature of the primer which was not touched by Bloomfield's approach is the writing exercises. Writing exercises are likely to be an effective addition to a primary program. " There is sufficient evidence in the research literature that integrating reading and writing may enhance reading achievement and children's understanding of the function of print. Through writing, children begin to develop a better understanding of the language concepts of reading, the terminology used to talk about print (e. g., letters, words, sentences), and that both reading and writing require the 'composition of meaning.'" (*Principles and Practices of Teaching Reading*, 6th Ed., Heilman, Blair, Rupley ; see also Chall, *op. cit.*, p. 171). The highly successful Montessori Reading Program utilizes the "trace and say" task sequences designed to teach the child to recognize and pronounce letter sounds and to use these in word recognition (Heilman, *et.al.*, *op. cit.*, p. 555). William C. Crain, cited in Flesch's *Why Johnny Still Can't Read*, observes that:

> Writing paves the way to reading. Through writing, children form a muscular and visual memory of the letters and words and therefore can recognize them. Consequently, the five or six-year-olds who have learned to write can usually learn to read with very little help from the teacher. Children often say that nobody taught them to read at all (p. 120).

Why a phonics approach to teaching adult non-readers how to read? For one thing, English is a phonetic language and is therefore susceptible to decoding. Had it not been for this singular feature, it would not even make sense to suggest phonics. Forgan puts the number of words in English that follow the phonetic principle at 85% (Forgan, *supra*); Flesch, citing the work of Hay and Wingo, among others, assigns a slightly higher value at 87% (*Why Johnny Can't Read*, 1955, p. 36). In his later book, *Why Johnny Still Can't Read* (pp. 94-96), he assigns the much higher value of 97.4%, citing the research done by Hanna, et. al. Even those who maintain that American English is non-phonetic at the phoneme-grapheme level, concede that it is more phonetic than most people realize at the morpho-phonemic level. (A phoneme is the smallest semantically functional unit of speech, whereas a morpheme is the smallest linguistic unit with a meaning of its own. Mazurkiewicz, *op. cit.*, p. 23.) More important, the Bishop experiment has shown that direct phonics instructions do benefit adult learners (Chall, *supra*). Further, Professor Chall, after sifting through research from the laboratory, the classroom and the clinic puts forward the qualified recommendation for a shift to a code emphasis in beginning reading method, though she does not recommend ignoring the practice of reading for meaning (Chall, *op. cit.*, p. 307).

This primer is divided into four main parts, which are further divided into sections. The first part of the primer introduces the learner to some sight words, and the letters of the alphabet and their sounds. The vowel sounds introduced at this stage are the long and the short, whether they are produced by single vowels or vowels in tandem. The learner is guided through the sounds produced by consonant-vowel combinations, and toward the end of part one, the learner finally hears other vowel sounds.

The sight words are enough in number to permit the construction of meaningful practice sentences. The beginning reader must learn the sight words first before going any further. The sight words are not illustrated because in a series of experiments, Dr. S. Jay Samuels has shown "that pictures not only don't help kids to learn whole words by look-and-say, but are an actual hindrance." Summarizing his findings, Dr. Samuels writes: "The bulk of the research findings on the effect of pictures on acquisition of a sight-vocabulary was that pictures interfere with learning to read" (Flesch, 1980, *op. cit.*, p. 47). The sight words, however, are introduced in a way that when read from left to right, they make a meaningful phrase or sentence. For instance, in Lesson 2, the sight words "are," "how," "you," and "all" are arranged "how-are-you-all" to express a meaning. It will be easier for the learner to learn and retain the words in this manner.

The keywords are illustrated. The illustrations are used as mnemonic devices to facilitate the learner's recognition, retention, and recall of the keywords. The keywords in turn facilitate recognition, retention and recall of the basic consonant-vowel combinations. These combinations constitute the "subskills" from which the learner can build his reading capacity.

The efficacy of this approach is documented by numerous studies. "The key-word method, by comparison, requires no rote learning at all and makes use of the mind's powerful ability to think in images. Numerous studies have shown that by forming a mental picture of something to be remembered, an impression is so firmly created in the brain that forgetting becomes virtually impossible." (D. Lewis and J. Greene, *op. cit.*, p. 181; see also *Brain Power*, Karl Albrecht, 1980, p. 28 and pp. 258-271).

No other exercise words or sentences are illustrated. The same experiments by Dr. Samuels showed that "pictures, when used as adjuncts to the printed texts, do not facilitate comprehension" (Flesch, 1980, *op. cit.*, p. 47).

There are two reasons for introducing two basic sounds initially. The first is to avoid confusing the learner. It will be easier for him to build a solid foundation if he deals only with two sounds. After the learner is thoroughly grounded on the long and short vowel sounds, he is introduced to other sounds. The second is that, in the long run, teaching the learner dual associations has greater transfer value than teaching him single associations.

The second part of the primer presents consonant blends and digraphs at the beginning of words; the third part presents consonant blends, digraphs, and various vowel-consonant combinations like "ous" and "ial" as word endings. The fourth contains reading materials in essay form.

This method of presentation was adopted on the theory that the learner will have an easier time learning if he proceeds from the simple to the more complex word structures. If he already knows how to read "ray" or "row," he is just a small step from reading "pray," "spray," "throw" and "growth." Further, as intimated above, it will be very confusing for the learner to come across letters or digraphs and blends which are constantly changing their function in a word. For instance, a learner will probably handle the various sounds associated with "gh" after he has thoroughly mastered the sounds associated with "g" and "f."

The method of presenting and teaching the second and third parts of the primer differs from the first. As usual the keywords are illustrated, but only to emphasize the consonant blend or digraph at the beginning, medial or end position in the word. At this time, the learner would have had enough phonics training to work out the exercise words and sentences with minimal assistance. Further phonics exercises would be superfluous. Phonics overdose is as dangerous as phonics underdose; care must be taken to administer the right amount (Chall, *op. cit.*, p. 163). "The optimum amount of phonics instruction for any learner is the minimum needed to become an independent reader" (Heilman, *et. al.*, *op. cit.*, p. 137). "Therefore, even in teaching decoding, meaning must always be the vitalizing and stabilizing factor. For this reason, form and meaning should be instantly fused into a single reaction: a direct interpretation of symbols into meaning. Thus the mind is freed from the burden of mechanics as much as possible, and forms become an almost invisible part of reading" (*Rx for Reading*, H. Grouse, 1986, p. 45). Further, "[e]xperiments have shown repeatedly that we remember meaningful associations best of all. Even arbitrary meaning helps memory more than no meaning. Inevitably, artificial memory systems that give meaning to something work better than the reminder strings of rote memory" (E. B. Blair, *op.cit.*, p. 104).

One careful study investigated ways of meaningful pairings. Subjects were divided into four groups and made to learn words in pairs. The first group learned by simply paying attention; the second group read the pairs, then read a sentence linking the pairs, for example, "Her hat fell into the bucket," for the hat/bucket pair; the third group read the pairs and then made up their own sentences to link the words; and the fourth group read the pairs and formed their visual images linking the words. A learner might imagine water being poured into a bucket from a hat, as an aid to remembering the hat/bucket pair. The results showed a progressive improvement in the recall average from the first group to the fourth. Using as the standard the first group's 5.57 recall average, it was found that the second group improved significantly, with 8.17; the third doubled the rate of the rote learners at 11.5; and the fourth group achieved a phenomenal amount of recall average at 13.1 items (*Ibid.*).

July 1990, Charleston, West Virginia

LETTER TO A TEACHER

Welcome to the E-Z Reader program. Today and in the next several days you will act as a guide. You will guide your student through the world of letters, their sounds, and the words and sentences they make. Your student will need a pencil and a notebook. He will better remember the things he saw and heard if he writes them down.

I would suggest that you make cardboard strips with consonants, consonant blends and digraphs written on them. I call them word diggers. They are easy to use. For example, take a word such as "bat." If the first letter is covered and a strip is slipped in front of "at", the student may uncover words such as "cat," "pat" and "spat." If the last letter is covered and a strip is slipped at the end of "ba," the student may be able to uncover words such as "bag," "bath" and "bald." Challenge and discovery make learning fun and exciting, and I am sure your student will enjoy the process. These are the physical tools you and your student need for your journey. First, however, I'll describe the world which you are about to explore.

The primer is divided into four parts. The first section covers consonants, sight words and vowel sounds. Initially, the student will study long and short vowel sounds. The least number of vowel sounds with which he deals in the beginning, the easier it is for him to master the subject matter. You will introduce him to other vowel sounds toward the end of Part One.

Your exercise words are presented in five columns. The left most column contains the "a" sounds. The "e," "i," "o" and "u" sounds will come in that order. After Part One, five other columns will be added to accommodate letters representing new sounds. This way the columns themselves will give the student a hint as to what sounds to expect.

Towards the end of Part One, there are two and three syllable practice words and some reading materials in essay form. The student is also introduced to suffixes, syllables added to base words to alter their meaning.

Part Two deals with consonant blends, digraphs and silent consonants at the beginning of words. Blends are letters in tandem that retain their distinctive sounds; digraphs produce one sound.

Part Three deals with blends, digraphs, silent consonants, and various syllables as word endings.

Part Four provides additional practice reading materials in essay form. They were placed last so that the student would not be obliged to read them before he felt ready to do so. As mentioned earlier, easier reading materials are provided toward the end of Part One.

You will start the lessons with the consonants, digraphs and sight words. The consonants are illustrated; the sight words are not. Sight words are those words that appear in the exercise sentences which were not introduced as keywords, such as "the," "likes" and "did." They will be used frequently in other lessons, and it can cause difficulties if the student proceeds without mastering them. Other sight words will be introduced as you go along.

It is a good idea to master each lesson before going to the next. Although you are absolutely free to adopt an approach suitable to you and your student, I would like to suggest this approach, to wit:

1. The student reads the keywords. The illustrations will help him recognize the words. If he has difficulty or is mistaken, help him. Make him sound out the basic phonetic sounds before reading the keyword. For instance, he should say "ah" then "apple" to make sure that he associates the two.

2. You and the student read the sight words, exercise words, and sentences together, or you read first and have him read after you.

3. The student reads the exercise words alone a second time (help him if necessary) and writes them down.

4. The student uses strips (word diggers) to try to discover new words. He writes down words which he discovers.

5. The student uses words in sentences. The list of words to be used in sentences serves as a

guide. The student may or may not use them. He may use as many words as he likes, including the words he discovered. He should write down the sentences. Ask the student to visualize his sentences. If his sentence is "I eat an apple," let him imagine that he is eating an apple. Visualizing will help him remember better. If the student can not write, write for him.

6. Review past lessons regularly. This will reinforce the learning process.

The student is not expected to know the meaning of all the words used in the primer. A glossary is provided at the end of the book. Teach him how to use it and introduce him to the use of the dictionary.

Thirty to forty minutes a day is just right for these exercises. As you go along, there may be times when your student can not focus on the subject matter, no matter how hard he tries. This is a signal for you to take a break. To proceed will only be counter-productive and frustrating. Rest. Relax, then go back to the lesson.

Before you begin, a few words of caution and advice.

Travel at your student's pace. Don't take anything for granted. The things you think are easy are a difficult task for him. Be patient, for patience can accomplish more than brilliance. Appreciate his effort, take pride in his progress, and be sure to let him know. After all, his accomplishment is yours, too!

Remember also that because of his condition, he may be sensitive. He may mistake an innocent frown for disapproval. This could set you back more than you know. Smile. Keep your sense of humor. Before you know it, your student has gone places and is off to the wonder world of printed words. Good luck!

LESSON 1 — CONSONANTS

Suggested approach for first two lessons (1 and 1.1):

1. Allow the student to read the keywords. Help out if he has difficulties or is mistaken.
2. Read sight words and practice sentences with the student or read them first and let the student read after you.
3. Let the student use words in sentences. The list of words to be used in sentences serves as a guide. The student may use as many words as he likes.

Formulate these rules and emphasize these observations:

1. C is hard when followed by A, O, U, and another consonant. It sounds like K. Stress the keywords.
2. C is soft when followed by E, I, or Y. It sounds like S. Stress the keywords.
3. G is hard when followed by A, O, and U. It represents the sound associated with "goat."
4. G is soft when followed by E, I, or Y. It represents the sound associated with "giant."
5. Stress the multiple or dual sounds of L, M, N, Q, R, S, and X. Show the student that although vowels control the sound that consonants make, L, M, N, R, and S make a sound closer to their sound in the alphabet when they are in the middle or end of a word.

LESSON 1.1

Follow the approach suggested for Lesson 1.

Formulate these rules and emphasize these observations:

1. When double C is followed by E or I, the first C sounds like K, the second sounds like S. "Success" and "accident" are good examples.
2. When double C is followed by O or U, it sounds like K. "Accordion" and "accuse" are good examples.
3. PH almost always sounds like F no matter what its position in the word.
4. A word can change its function by changing its position in a sentence, thus changing the sense of the sentence, too. This is an important aspect of the lessons, and you must make sure that the student understands these changes by discussing the sentences as they occur in the lessons.

LESSON 2

Suggested approach to Lessons 2 to 43:

1. Allow the student to read the keywords. If he is mistaken or having difficulty, help him. Make him sound out the basic phonetic sound before reading the keyword. For instance, the student should say "ah" before saying "apple." This will insure that he will associate the two.

2. Read the sight words, exercise words and sentences with the student, or read them first, having the student read after you.

3. The student reads the exercise words by himself and writes them down.

4. The student uses strips (word diggers) and tries to discover new words from the exercise words. You can help him by giving him clues. He writes down words he discovers.

5. The student uses words in sentences. The list of words to be used in sentences will serve as a guide.

He can use as many words as he likes, including the ones he may have discovered. He should write down his sentences. If he can not write, you may write down the sentences for him.

Encourage him to visualize his sentences. For instance, if the sentence is "I eat an apple," let him imagine eating an apple. He will remember and recall better this way.

Since the student is not expected to know the meaning of all the words in the reading book, a glossary is provided for reference. Teach him how to use the glossary and a dictionary.

After the exercises, go back to the keywords. For instance, choose the word "apple." Say it: /ap/p'l/. Introduce him to the syllable. Tell him a syllable is a word or part of a word that is pronounced with one uninterrupted voice. Go back to "apple." Say it again for emphasis.

Formulate and emphasize these rules:

1. Every syllable has only one vowel sound. A word, therefore, will have as many syllables as there are vowel sounds.

2. A double consonant will divide in the middle. Note /ap/p'l/ and /um/brel/la/.

3. P + le and like endings, for example b + le or g + le are separate syllables.

4. When dividing a word into syllables, always start from the end of the word. (Try syllabicating a few exercise words with the learner).

LESSON 3

Follow the approach suggested for Lesson 2.

LESSON 4

Follow the approach suggested for Lesson 2.

Formulate and emphasize the **TWO VOWEL RULE** as follows: When there are two consecutive vowels in a word or syllable, the first usually represents a long sound and the second is silent. Stress that the rule does not hold true in every case but in Part One of the book, it is a useful rule to remember.

LESSON 5

Follow the approach suggested for Lesson 2.

Stress the fact that the OE form does not appear very frequently, but it is important to study it because it frequently appears in the O + consonant + E form, as in "hope."

LESSON 6

Follow the approach suggested for Lesson 2.

Now that you have completed Lessons 4, 5, and 6, repeat the Two Vowel Rule: When two vowels go together the first represents the long sound and the second is silent.

Re-state that this is not always the case and that there are times when the vowels are pronounced separately.

Give him this pointer: When he meets vowels in tandem, he should try sounding them together first. If he can not determine the word, then sound them out separately. Ask him to give you words containing vowels in tandem which do not form part of one syllable. You can give him these clues:

1. one who writes verses (poet)
2. a car needs it to run (fuel)
3. two singers singing together (duet)
4. a formal fight to end a quarrel (duel)
5. to follow a winding course (meander)

Let him write down his answers.

LESSON 7

Follow the approach suggested for Lesson 2.

Stress the fact that Y is a consonant which functions also as a vowel. A simple test determines if it functions as a vowel: when Y follows a consonant and is not a separate syllable, it is always used as a vowel. To emphasize the test, call his attention to the words "banyan," b-a-n-y-a-n, and "canyon," c-a-n-y-o-n, in which Y follows N, a consonant, but it is not used as a vowel because it begins a syllable.

LESSON 7.1

Follow the approach suggested for Lesson 2.

LESSON 7.2

Follow the approach suggested for Lesson 2.

Formulate and emphasize the following rules:

1. When Y concludes a one-syllable word like "by" or "cry," it usually represents the sound of the long I. Reiterate: A syllable is a word or part of a word that is pronounced with a single, uninterrupted voice. The keyword "cymbals" is divided into two syllables: cym and bals. So is "baby," which is divided into /bay/ and /bee/.

2. When Y is followed by the letter E, whether immediately as in "dye" or after a consonant, as in "type," Y usually represents the sound of long I.

3. When Y concludes a word with two or more syllables, it usually represents the long E sound. However, there are cases when Y represents the long I sound as in "deny," "rely," "imply," "lullaby" and "supply." Try the long E sound first.

4. When Y occurs in a closed syllable like "gyp" in "gypsy" or in a word like "gym," Y usually represents the short I sound. As a reminder, a closed syllable is one that ends with a consonant.

LESSON 8

Follow the approach suggested for Lesson 2.

Formulate and emphasize the following rules:

1. The sound associated with the short vowel is usually produced when a single vowel word or syllable ends in a consonant. Point to the keywords.

2. When a syllable or word ends in a vowel, the sound produced is usually that of the long vowel. This is true of a single vowel syllable, as in /i/bis or /o/pen.

3. When a word or syllable ends in E and is separated from another vowel by a consonant, as in "bone" or "bike," the E is silent and the first vowel represents the long sound. Call this the **E ENDING RULE**. Point out that this rule applies to Y when Y is used as a vowel.

4. Reiterate: When a word or syllable has two consecutive vowels, as in "boat," "/oat/meal" or "nail," what is heard is the long sound of the first vowel, the second being silent. This is the TWO VOWEL RULE.

5. The word "oatmeal" brings in a useful syllabication rule. When dealing with compound words, always divide them into their component words. Thus, "oatmeal" divides into /oat/meal/.

Ask your student to give you examples of compound words. Let him use each one in a sentence as part of the writing exercises.

LESSON 9

Follow the approach suggested for Lesson 2.

Reiterate and emphasize the following rules:

1. When C is followed by vowels A, O or U, C represents the sound of K. An exception, "facade" (/fa/sad/), means the face of a building.
2. C represents the K sound when it is at the end of a word like "mimic" or "magic" or a syllable, as in pic/nic.
3. C also represents the K sound when it is followed by a consonant, as in "act".
4. When the consonant is another C + E, I or Y, the double C sounds like KS. Point out "success."
5. When double C is followed by O or U, it sounds like K. Point out "accordion" and "accuse."

LESSON 10

Follow the suggested approach for Lesson 2.

Repeat and emphasize the following rules:

1. When C is followed by E, I or Y, C produces the sound associated with S, as in Sinbad. (At this point you may want to ask the student about the rule on double C.)
2. When a word has the VOWEL-CONSONANT-CONSONANT-VOWEL form, as in the keyword "cymbals," you must divide between the consonants to form syllables: /cym/bals/. Point out the difference between "cymbals" and "cyclone". "Cyclone" does not divide between "c" and "l" because CL is a consonant blend. Consonant blends usually stay in one syllable.

LESSON 11

Follow the approach suggested for Lesson 2.

Formulate and emphasize the following rules:

1. When two alike consonants appear together, as in "doll" and "dill", the first is sounded and the second is silent. This is true of all twin consonants from BB to ZZ. Cite exceptions: When CC is followed by E or I, the first C sounds like K and the second C sounds like S as in accident.
   In some cases when ZZ is followed by a vowel, the sound of ZZ is like TS as in "pizza."
   The second G in "suggest" is sometimes pronounced as J, as in /sug/jest/.
2. When C and K appear in tandem as in "duck", they produce the sound associated with K. Another way of saying it, is that C is silent.

LESSON 12

Follow the approach suggested for Lesson 2.

Call the student's attention to the word "focus." Introduce him to the "schwa" sound or the unstressed vowel in the syllable "cus". The schwa sound is represented by the inverted E sign.

LESSON 13

Follow the approach suggested for Lesson 2.

Reiterate and emphasize the following rule:

1. When G is followed by A, O, U or another consonant, it represents the sound associated with "goat." This is the hard G sound. "Margarine" and "hangar," an aircraft shed, are exceptions.
2. G followed by E, I or Y usually represents the sound of J, as in "giant".

LESSON 14

Follow the approach suggested for Lesson 2.

Reiterate and emphasize the following rules:

1. When G is followed by E, I or Y, it usually takes the sound associated with J, as in "jump." Point out that in some instances — as shown in the previous lesson — G, even when

followed by E and I, retains the hard G sound, as in "geese," "get" and "gift." Try the J sound first.

2. The observation above becomes almost certain when GE, GI or GY is located in the middle or at the end of a word.

Point out the sound of G in "age," "magi" and "edgy."

Point out the sound of IE in the keyword "genie." It is an exception to the two vowel rule because the first vowel is not heard.

LESSON 15

Follow the approach suggested for Lesson 2.

Point out that in "honor," "honest," "hour" or "heir," the H is always silent, but in "herb," the word may be pronounced with or without the H.

LESSON 16

Follow the approach suggested for Lesson 2.

LESSON 17

Follow the approach suggested for Lesson 2.

(This may be a good time to do syllabication and review some of the syllabication rules.)

Emphasize this observation:

When A is found at the end of a word, it almost never has the long sound. Give the following words as examples: Ali Baba, Mecca, banana, alfalfa, mama, mesa, regatta. A is an exception to the rule that a vowel at the end of a word usually represents the long sound.

You can ask the student to give you his own examples if he can. Help him write down his examples.

LESSON 18

Follow the approach suggested for Lesson 2.

Emphasize the schwa sound of O in "lemon" and of U in "locust."

LESSON 19

Follow the approach suggested for Lesson 2.

Pick out the keywords "music" and "medic" and point out the common configuration, VOWEL-CONSONANT-VOWEL(VCV). Point out that they divide into syllables differently. "Music" divides into /mu/sic/ while "medic" divides into /med/ic/. Half of the time when one sees words with the form V-C-V, such words will divide as "music" does. The student should first try dividing a word as "music" is divided. If the word can not be determined, he should try dividing as "medic" is divided.

LESSON 20

Follow the approach suggested for Lesson 2.

LESSON 21

Follow the approach suggested for Lesson 2.

(This is a good time to do syllabication exercises. Reiterate the rules which state that compound words divide into root words ("pumpkin" divides into "pump" and "kin") and that double consonants divide in the middle as "panda" and "pencil" do (/pan/da/ and /pen/cil/).

LESSON 22

Follow the approach suggested for Lesson 2.

Emphasize the following observations:

1. In the initial position, QU is pronounced with the KW sound. Exceptions are: "quay" (kee), meaning a docking and landing place; "quatrefoil" (katerfoil), meaning a leaf with four leaflets; "Quito" (keeto), the Capital of Ecuador.

2. In the end position, QUE is almost always pronounced as K. One exception is risque (ris/kay), a French-lent word meaning daring.

3. In the medial position of most French, Latin and other foreign-lent words, QUE represents the sound of K.

LESSON 23

Follow the approach suggested for Lesson 2.

LESSON 24

Before tackling lessons 24, 25 and 26, explain to your student the importance of these lessons. Ordinarily, the vowels control the sounds of consonants with which they are placed. In the case of the consonant R, however, it is R which controls the sound of the vowels in a good number of cases.

Follow the approach suggested for Lesson 2.

LESSON 25

Make the following observations before tackling this lesson, to wit:

1. The O before R usually represents the half O sound associated with the diphthong AU. This is the sound you hear in "for" (as in for me), "ore" (as in gold ore), and "orbit" (as in lunar orbit).

2. A before R usually represents one or the other of two sounds. AH as in car, far, father, is very frequently used. The other sound is heard AIR as in care and bare.

3. E, I or U before R represents the same sound. Listen: her shoes, fir tree, fur coat.

4. When vowels are separate syllables, they are not R-controlled, for example o/rate, i/rate, and U/ranus.

Follow the approach suggested for Lesson 2, but omit Step 1.

LESSON 26

Follow the approach suggested for Lesson 2, but omit Step 1.

LESSON 27

Follow the approach suggested for Lesson 2.

LESSON 28

Explain that the second part of the lesson on the consonant S covers instances when S produces the Z sound, as in fuse, and the SH sound as in sugar. The ZH sound, as in television, will be taken up in another lesson. Though there are not many words that fall into these categories, they are nonetheless commonly used words with which everyone should at least be acquainted. Start with the Z sound first, then go to the SH sound. Before you do, make these observations:

1. When S is found at the beginning of a word, the sound it represents is S, as in Santa. Only in the words sugar and sure and their derivatives does S take the SH sound.

2. When S is found at the end of a word, it usually represents the sound of Z if it is a morpheme or an inflectional ending or if it follows an accented or voiced vowel. In buds, hugs and ranks, S is a morpheme in that it is the smallest part of a word which conveys meaning: in this case, "more than one." In goes or hers, it is an inflectional ending in that S signals a change in the grammatical sense of the word. We will study these two cases in more detail later. In his or as, S follows a voiced or accented sound, so it represents Z.

3. In any other case, when S is at the middle or the end of a word, it will sound like itself in the alphabet. Remind the student of "bus." Try "mascot" when S is at the middle. Also, when S forms part of a blend, it sounds itself, as in "snake."

Follow the approach suggested for Lesson 2, but omit Step 1.

LESSON 29

Follow the approach suggested for Lesson 2.

LESSON 30

Follow the approach suggested for Lesson 2.

LESSON 31

Follow the approach suggested for Lesson 2.

LESSON 32

Point out that X has several sounds associated with it. Significantly, it has no distinctive sound of its own. The two most common sounds are KS, as in "ax," and GZ, as in "exit." Less common are the Z sounds as in "xylophone" and KZH or GZH, as in luGZHury or lukZHUry (for luxury). Both pronunciations are correct. In the word "obnoxious," X takes the KSH sound, and in S-i-o-u-x, /soo/, X is silent — a non-sound.

Follow the approach suggested for Lesson 2.

LESSONS 33 and 33.1

Follow the approach suggested for Lesson 2. Omit Step 1.

LESSON 34

Follow the approach suggested for Lesson 2.

Emphasize that as a rule, Y functions as a consonant when it is at the beginning of a word or a syllable and it is followed by a vowel. In "canyon," Y begins a syllable and is followed by a vowel.

LESSON 35

Follow the approach suggested for Lesson 2.

LESSON 36

Follow the approach suggested for Lesson 2.

LESSON 37

Before tackling this lesson, remind your student that all Gs and GHs in the first column are silent.

Follow the approach suggested for Lesson 2.

Make these observations:

1. "Guide" and the exercise words follow the E ending rule but not the two vowel rule, which means that the E at the end is silent and the I represents the long sound.
   Had "guide" followed the two vowel rule, U would talk and I would be silent.
2. The same thing is true of the exercise words in the column under the keyword "field." As long as they end in E, they follow the E ENDING RULE. In "field," we hear the second vowel "talking," an exception to our TWO VOWEL RULE.

LESSON 38

You come now to vowel combinations that represent the short vowel sounds. Because the first vowel does not represent the long sound, these combinations are called variant vowel digraphs. Note that in the case of U + I in guitar and O + U in couple, the first vowel is silent, and the second vowel does the "talking." This is the second set of exceptions to the two vowel rule.

Before you proceed with the lesson, remind your student that GHs this time are pronounced as F.

Follow the approach suggested for Lesson 2.

LESSON 39

Explain that in the following exercises, when the letter A is followed by U, W and L, it produces a sound half way between the long and the short O sound.

Follow the approach suggested for Lesson 2.

LESSON 40

Explain that this section is divided into 4 lessons. The first two lessons deal with the long and short double O sounds and the last two deal with diphthongs. Diphthongs are two vowel sounds joined in one syllable to form one speech sound. The first lesson will deal with the long and short double O sounds.

Follow the approach suggested for Lesson 2.

LESSON 41

Explain that this is an extension of the previous lessons. This time however, the long double O sound will come from U, UE, UI, EW and OU, and the short double O sound will come from the letter O.

Make this observation:

1. When E + W is after R, L, J, S or CH, it usually represents the long double O sound; if it follows any other letter, it usually represents the long U sound.

This observation holds well when U, UI, UE or U + consonant + E follows R, L, J, S or CH. Point out the words "ruby," "juice," "blue" and "super."

Follow the approach suggested for Lesson 2.

LESSON 42

Follow the approach suggested for Lesson 2.

LESSON 43

Follow the approach suggested for Lesson 2.

LESSON 44

1. Allow the student to read the exercise words. Help when necessary.
2. Let him construct sentences of his own, using the list of words. The list serves as a guide, and he may use as many words as he likes.
3. Let the student read practice reading materials in the lesson. Give help when it is needed.

LESSON 45

Before you and your student go any further, it is necessary to introduce him to suffixes. Suffixes are word endings that change the meaning of the words to which they are added.

Although there are many, you will cover only **ING, ER, ED, ES, S, EST** and **EN**. Before taking up the rules, make the following general observations, to wit:

1. **S** and **ES** are added only to nouns (name words), pronouns (substitutes to name words), and verbs (action words). When either is added to a noun (name word), it changes the meaning of the noun from one to more than one. This applies to all name words that name persons, places, or things. When the name word ends in S, X, Z, O, SH, or CH, the suffix **ES** is added instead of **S**. In the word house, S is added to make it houses; in the word mass, the suffix **ES** is added to make it masses. In both cases the additions change the meaning from one to more than one.

2. When **S** is added to a pronoun or noun substitute, the suffix S shows possession. Point out ours, theirs, yours.

3. When **S** or **ES** is added to verbs or action words, the addition of S or ES tells us who is (are) the doer or doers of the action. It will also tell you that the action is presently taking place. When the person speaking does the action or many are doing the action, the verb will not end in S or ES. In any other case, add the suffix S or ES. Point out "I go," "they go," "Peter and Paul go," "he goes," "she goes," "it goes," "Mary goes," and "dogs go."

4. The suffixes **ING, ED** and **EN** are added to verbs or action words to signify a change in verb tense or the time when the action takes place. Give examples: "You are listening right now" (signifying the present). "You listened yesterday" or "I have given up smoking" (signifying a past action).

5. The suffixes **ER** and **EST** are added only to what we call adverbs (words that modify the meaning of verbs or other adverbs, adjectives, noun modifiers or picture words). These suffixes indicate comparative degrees in the relationship between two or more persons or

things. The suffix **ER** refers to a comparison between two or more persons or things. The suffix **EST** refers to a comparison among three or more persons or things. Give examples — first: "Peter is happier than Alan"; second: "Of the three, Peter is the happiest."

6. The suffix **S** at the end of words should not be mistaken for the apostrophe **S** at the end of name words as in Peter's or Paul's or Mary's, showing possession. After pronouns, the apostrophe **S** indicates that a part of an action word has been omitted: **there** apostrophe **S** means "there is"; **it** apostrophe **S** means "it is."

7. The suffix **ED** is a separate syllable only if it follows the letters t and d, but not any other. Point out /want/ed, /goad/ed/, /raid/ed/. (You can let your student try other words for emphasis).

8. Suffixes (and prefixes) are separate syllables. In dividing a word into syllables, the suffixes (and prefixes) should be separated first.

The first rule is: When adding ING to a base word ending in E, drop the vowel E and add the suffix ING.

like = lik + ing = liking   make = mak + ing = making
joke = jok + ing = joking   line = lin + ing = lining

The same is true when suffixes that begin with E like ED; ER; ES are added:

like = lik + ed = liked   make = mak + er = maker
joke = jok + es = jokes   line = lin + es = lines

Let the student work on the exercises. (Do the exercises and check the answers on page 66.)

The second rule is: When the last three letters have the consonant-vowel-consonant pattern like the words cut, gag, hit and debug, the final consonant is doubled before adding the suffixes.

cut = cutt + ing = cutting   gag = gagg + ed = gagged
hit = hitt + ing = hitting   debug = debugg + ed = debugged

Let the student work on the exercises. (Do the exercises and check the answers on page 66.)

There is an exception. When the last three letters have the consonant-vowel-consonant pattern, but the last letter is Y, do not double the Y. Add **ING, ER, ED** and **S** to the root words. Let's try some:

play = play + ing = playing   play = play + er = player
play = play + ed = played   play = play + s = plays

Let the student work on the exercises. (Do the exercises and check the answers on page 66.)

The third rule is: When the base words end in a consonant but do not fall into the consonant-vowel-consonant pattern, add suffixes without changing the spelling of the base words.

feed = feed + er = feeder   add = add + ing = adding
fish = fish + es = fishes   eat = eat + en = eaten

Let the student work on the exercises. (Do the exercises and check the answers on page 66.)

The fourth rule is: When the last letter is Y and it is preceded by a consonant, the Y in the base word is changed into **I** before adding the suffixes.

dry = dr + i + ed = dried   jelly = jell + i + es = jellies·
cry = cr + i + er = crier   soggy = sogg + i + est = soggiest

The suffix ING is simply added to the root word in appropriate cases as in:

dry = dry + ing = drying   cry = cry + ing = crying

Let the student work on the exercises. (Do the exercises and check the answers on page 66.)

LESSON 46

Beginning with this section, there will be five additional columns below the regular columns. They will be separated by a line. The first and second columns will contain the diphthong sounds associated with **house** and **oyster**, respectively; the third column contains the half-way O sound associated with **auto**; the fourth, the short double O sound associated with **book**; the fifth, the long double O sound associated with **moose**. In this and a few succeeding lessons, a headline is provided as a guide. After the student is used to the sounds associated with the new columns, the headline will be removed.

At this point, the student should be able to read. Even if he is not reading as efficiently as might be expected, he should be reading well enough to warrant a change in the approach to the lessons.

The suggested approach at this point:

1. Allow the student to read keywords and all the exercises. Help when necessary.
2. The student uses strips (word diggers) to discover new words. He writes down the new words.
3. The student uses words in sentences. The list of words to be used in sentences serves as a guide. He may use as many words as he likes, including those which he may have discovered.
4. The student may be introduced to the reading materials in Part Four of the book. At this point, the student should be encouraged to bring to the sessions reading materials in which he is interested. He can read them as part of the exercises.

Some important observations to make in this lesson:

1. O followed by LD or LT almost always produces the long O sound.
2. I followed by LD has a 50-50 chance of producing the long I sound.
3. The GE combination — whether occurring at the end or at the medial position in a word — is almost always pronounced as J.
4. When a word ends in E but is preceded by two consecutive consonants, the final E may be silent *but it will not make the sound of the preceding vowel long.* Call this the **SECOND E ENDING Rule.**
5. Generally, consonant blends and digraphs stay together in one syllable. Remind student of /cy/clone/.

LESSON 47

Follow the approach suggested for Lesson 46.
Point out the short U sound in flood. Blood and flood and their derivatives are probably the only words of the double O form that have the short U sound.

LESSON 48

Follow the approach suggested for Lesson 46.
Point out the last word in the upper second column of the PL blends. EA is a variant digraph and represents the short E sound. S represents the ZH sound. Say it: /plezh/er/. Also, point out the last word in the upper first column of the SL blend. The EI is pronounced as long A and the GH is silent. Say it: /slay/. You will see many examples like this in these lessons.

LESSON 49

Follow the approach suggested for Lesson 46.

LESSON 50

Follow the approach suggested for Lesson 46.
Point out the last word in the upper column one. What is heard is the long A sound of the EA combination. Say it: /brayk/.

LESSON 51

Follow the approach suggested for Lesson 46.
Call attention to the last word in the upper column one. It is important in two senses:

1. It is read "draft" and is probably one of the only three words of the AU form with the short A sound. Remind the student of "aunt" and "laugh".
2. Almost always, GH is silent when followed by T. "Draft" is probably the only exception.

LESSON 52

Follow the approach suggested for Lesson 46.
Point out the first word in the upper first column of the GR blends. Again, we have an instance of EA sounding like a long A. Say it: /grayt/. Point out also that the first word in the upper second column is an exception to the two-vowel rule. Let the student hear how the second vowel does the "talking" with the long sound, /greef/.

LESSON 53

Follow the approach suggested for Lesson 46.

Two words bear special attention — the last two in the upper second column. In both, EA represents the short E sound; in the latter, S represents the ZH sound. Say it: /tred/ and /tre/zher/.

LESSON 54

Follow the approach suggested for Lesson 46.

LESSON 55

Follow the approach suggested for Lesson 46.

Call attention to "skew" and "skewer" under the U-column. Remind the student of the rule: EW following L, R, S, J and CH almost always represents the long double O sound, but following any other consonant, it almost always represents the long U sound. The two words reinforce the rule.

LESSON 56

Follow the approach suggested for Lesson 46.

LESSON 57

Follow the approach suggested for Lesson 46.

LESSON 58

Follow the approach suggested for Lesson 46.

LESSON 59

Follow the approach suggested for Lesson 46.

Point out the first word of the upper first column of the ST blends. The EA combination has a long A sound, /stayk/.

LESSON 60

Follow the approach suggested for Lesson 46.

Point out that GU is not a consonant blend, but the sound it produces is the sound associated with GW. Hence, it is included here.

LESSON 61

Follow the approach suggested for Lesson 46.

Point out that most writers classify CH, PH, SH, TH and WH as regular digraphs. Strictly speaking, only SH should be considered regular, because no matter where it is located in a word or what letters follow it, it represents one sound. The same can not be said of the rest. They are irregular.

You will start this section with the two sounds which CH represents. The third sound associated with CH, represented in the word "chevron" will be taken up with the digraph SH. Emphasize the following:

1. The most common sound associated with CH is represented in the word chair. You should always try this sound first. If this does not work, try the K sound. If both fail, you can try the SH sound.
2. When CH comes before a consonant like R or L, it always represents the K sound
3. C-h-o-i-r = choir; church choir is worth mentioning. Note the KW sound of the digraph CH and the long I sound of the tandem OI.

LESSON 62

Follow the approach suggested for Lesson 46.

LESSON 63

Follow the approach suggested for Lesson 46.

Emphasize the following:

1. When the word is of French origin, the digraph CH is almost always pronounced with the SH sound, no matter where it may be located. The words "brochure," "cache," and "chef" are some examples.

LESSON 64

Follow the approach suggested for Lesson 46.

Emphasize that in the initial position, TH is voiced only in the instances indicated in the exercise words. All others are voiceless.

LESSON 65

Follow the approach suggested for Lesson 46.

LESSON 66

Follow the approach suggested for Lesson 46.

This lesson completes the lessons on the sounds of GH. Emphasize these observations:

1. When GH is in the initial position in a word, H is always silent and it represents the hard G sound.
2. When GH is followed by T, whether it is in the medial or end position, it is usually silent. D-r-a-u-g-h-t = draft; its derivatives are probably the only exceptions.
3. When the single letter I is followed by GH or GHT, GH is always silent, and I represents the long sound. Give some examples: night, light, right.
4. In a few words, GH represents the F sound. You have covered most, if not all of them in a previous lesson. Remind the student of the words "tough," "rough," "enough."
5. The G in the GN combination is always silent, no matter where it is located in a word. In a few French and Italian-borrowed words like "bologna" (also read as balony) and "mignon," meaning small and pretty, the GN represents the sound of Y. Note though, that when G and N are part of separate syllables, as in "malignant," both G and N are pronounced, although in "malign" (the root word), G is silent.
6. The K in the KN combination is always silent at the beginning of words.

LESSON 67

Follow the approach suggested for Lesson 46.

Emphasize the following:

1. P is silent when it appears before any consonant in the initial position, except H. PH is pronounced as F.
2. Two interesting but very rare cases are: "pfennig" (an old German coin), in which P is silent before F, and "phthisis" (tuberculosis), in which PH is silent before TH.
3. The H after R is always silent in whatever position RH is found. H after K is also silent in the KH combination.

LESSON 68

Follow the approach suggested for Lesson 46.

LESSON 69

Follow the approach suggested for Lesson 46.

LESSON 70

Follow the approach suggested for Lesson 46.

Formulate and emphasize the following rules:

1. O followed by LD or LT almost always produces the long O sound.
2. I followed by LD has a 50-50 chance of producing the long I sound. Try the long I first.
3. The GE combination, whether occurring at the end of the word or in the medial position, usually represents the sound of J.

4. When a word ends in E but is preceded by two consecutive consonants, the final E may be silent, but it will not make the sound of the preceding vowel long. You will find many applications of this rule in this and the succeeding lessons. Call this the SECOND E ENDING RULE.

5. Generally, consonant blends and digraphs stay together in one syllable. Remind the student of /cy/clone/.

LESSON 71

Follow the approach suggested for Lesson 46.

Emphasize the following observations:

1. NX is pronounced as NKS, as in "lynx."

2. The combinations NCE and NSE produce the same sound, the sound associated with NS. E is silent at the end.

Formulate and stress the following rules:

1. I followed by NT usually produces the short I sound. Probably the only exception is "pint," as in pint of milk.

2. I followed by ND almost always produces the long I sound. Probably the only exceptions are: wind, as in cold wind, and rescind, as in rescind a contract.

3. Reiterate the rule that when double C is followed by E or I, the first C represents the K sound and the second C represents the S sound.

LESSON 72

Follow the approach suggested for Lesson 46.

Emphasize the following observations:

1. The RGE combination is pronounced RJ, as in "barge."

2. The combination RCE and RSE produce the sound associated with RS, as in "horse."

3. A reminder: The letters E, I or U before R produce the same sound. Remind the student of the words "her," "fir" and "fur."

LESSON 73

Follow the approach suggested for Lesson 46.

Emphasize the following observations:

1. O or OA, immediately followed by ST, is usually associated with the long O sound. "Cost" and "lost" are exceptions. Try the long O first.

2. When the STE combination follows A or O, A or O represent the long sound.

LESSON 74

Emphasize the following observation: The combination CONSONANT + LE forms a syllable, and the LE represents the sound of half U + L. (In most Webster's Dictionaries, it is CONSONANT + 'l to indicate a voice glide.)

Follow the approach suggested for Lesson 46.

LESSON 75

Follow the approach suggested for Lesson 46.

LESSON 76

You come now to consonant digraphs as word endings. Some writers classify CH, TH, SH and NG as regular digraphs, classifying the rest as "other" digraphs. That classification pattern is not followed here. One reason is that CH is not regular. Sometimes it represents the K sound, as in "ache"; sometimes it represents the SH sound, as in "chef." TH is irregular, too. Point out: "Take a bath" and "bathe the baby." The first is voiceless TH; the second is the voiced TH. For this reason, they are treated here in alphabetical order.

Emphasize: TH + E at the very end of a word signals the voiced TH.

Follow the approach suggested for Lesson 46.

LESSON 77

Follow the approach suggested for Lesson 46.

LESSON 78

At times two consonants make one sound, even though they are not digraphs. They make one sound because one is silent. You will take up the more common consonant combinations where one or both consonants are silent. Some rare, silent consonants are also covered by the lesson.

Follow the approach suggested for Lesson 46.

LESSON 79

Follow the approach suggested for Lesson 46.

LESSON 80

Follow the approach suggested for Lesson 46.

LESSON 81

Follow the approach suggested for Lesson 46.

Emphasize this observation: UE after G at the end position in words is usually silent, but this is not always the case. "Ague," /a/gyoo/ (a shivering fit) and "dengue," /deng/gay/ (a disease borne by mosquitoes) are notable exceptions.

LESSON 82

At last you are home! We have reserved for you and your student the most irregular words there are, as far as pronunciation is concerned. The words are foreign words, mostly French, that have been adopted in the English language. They are commonly used, and it pays to know how to read them. Since the words are not pronounced as they are spelled, knowing the words themselves and how to read them is the best way to handle them.

Follow the approach suggested for Lesson 46.

After finishing Lesson 82, the following observations may be made, to wit:

1. When a word of French origin ends in the letter T or R and is preceded by the letter E, the T or the R is silent and the E represents the long A sound. Two words which show that this is not always the case are: bang/kwit/, "banquet," and /boo/ton/yer/, "boutonniere" (a flower worn on the buttonhole).

2. The letter E or double E at the end of the words of French origin is usually pronounced with the long A sound. Showing that this is not always the case, note /mar/kee/, "marquee" (a roof-like projection in front of a theater).

3. S and X at the end of French-borrowed words are usually silent. Point out "Mardi Gras," "Grand Prix" and "debris."

4. The GE in French-borrowed words have the ZH sound rather than the J sound associated with English words.

5. The IE at the end of the word is sometimes pronounced with the long I sound as in pie, and sometimes with the short I sound, as in the exercise words. IE is pronounced with the short I sound when it signifies: (a) smallness, as in "lassie" or "Debbie"; (b) a change in the number of a word ending in Y, like candy to candies or baby to babies; (c) the word is a foreign-lent word, such as "genie" (which is French) or "cowrie" (which is Hindu).

EPILOGUE

The author of this primer cannot hope and did not attempt to cover all the phonic, syllabication and pronunciation rules and exceptions to the rules. There are many, and it serves no useful purpose to clutter the mind with so much when the net result could be to confuse, rather than help. What I tried to do was to cover what I thought were the most useful rules to remember and alert you to their exceptions, if there were any.

You may think that the rules are quite capricious and whimsical. For instance, you will probably ask: " Why does the letter I sound short in bikini and long in alumni, when both of them end in NI?" "Why should E be sounding off so loudly in abalone and Comanche, when it is supposed to be silent according to our two-E-ending rules?" Actually, there is a perfectly logical answer to these questions. The words were borrowed; when they were adopted by American English, they retained their respective pronunciations. "Bikini" came from a Pacific atoll of the same name; "abalone" came from Spanish and "Comanche" came from Mexican-Spanish. Not all exceptions have a simple explanation, but there is a reason for them, and knowing the rules and their exceptions will certainly help you in decoding new words which you will meet along your way.

Neither can this primer cover all the sounds that the letters of the alphabet make, alone or in combinations. It is safe to say that we have covered more than 90% of those sounds. I am confident that what little ground we have not explored, you can now very easily cover on your own.

The emphasis of this primer has been on the long and short vowel sounds, whether the vowel acts alone or goes in tandem. As we have seen, when two vowels go together, the first talks and the second takes a walk, as some say. In bead, E talks and A takes a walk. In boat, it is again A's turn to take a walk while O, the first vowel, does the talking.

There are times, though, when the second vowel is more talkative and the first, in deference, becomes silent. Thus, in the word believe, I yields to E, which says its piece. Perhaps the first vowel welcomes with relief the times when the second becomes talkative. Vowels in tandem cover a wide field, and to be talking all the time can be tiresome. So in guise, guild, build and eider and Einstein, U and E permit I to do all the talking. In phoenix and Phoebe, E again does the talking. In amoeba, there really is not much space for both of them, so E takes center stage, while O stays in the wings.

There are times, though, when both get tired and lazy. They hang around but simply refuse to talk! It is right for U and E to be quiet inside a mosque or at a meeting of the League of Nations, but to utter not a word or a squeak at a burlesque show is perhaps a little grotesque. In monologue, their silence is well understood. But must they also be quiet in a dialogue or harangue? Is it pique? Or is it fatigue that makes them quiet? Have they lost their tongues? Hardly! In duet, they duel to be heard; so both are heard. In fuel and gruel, both speak up again, though in feud, E gives way to U, perhaps, to keep the peace! In Europe and euphoria, they speak with one voice again.

Whatever it is that keeps both of them quiet at times puzzles and intrigues because we know that E and U are not only talkative, but also are extremely fond of imitating the sounds that other letters make. They assume their best French accent when they talk about past-on decor (applique — ap/li/kay) or against indecent (risque — ris/kay) movies. Even when suffering from severe pain, rashes and fever (dengue — den/gay), they cannot help imitating the sound that long A makes.

E, alone or in cooperation with others, never tires of imitating the sound of long A: eight, obey, ballet, cafe, and matinee are just a few. Occasionally, it mimics the sound of short A. Listen — entree, envelope, and an encore, too! In fact, with the help of W, E does a very good imitation of U in few.

Not to be outdone, U, with Y, mimics the sound of long I in buy and guy (a thing E cannot do) and does a perfect long double O sound in ruby, tuna and super (a thing E, with W, does well, too!). U is so irrepressible sometimes that not even a shivering fit (ague — /ay/gyoo/), can make it keep quiet.

Whatever the reason is for the silence of U and E — and for that matter, of the other letters of the alphabet at one time or another — one thing is certain: When they speak to us in words and sentences, they can transport us to a world of magic and fantasy; they can thrill and enthrall, give aid and comfort, encourage, exhort, soothe a wound, ease a pain, inform and educate, give directions or issue warnings, converse, amuse, entertain or, simply, tickle a funny bone.

I am confident that this primer has given your student the necessary tools to function as a beginning reader. It is my hope, as it is the hope of those who helped me in preparing it, that I have aroused in beginning adult readers the desire to explore further the world of the written word — in papers, in magazines or in books. That world is waiting. The student can now explore it and discover its beauty, its endless variety, its inexhaustible wealth in gems of thought and ideas. There are a very few things in the world that could match the utility, the excitement, and the pleasures of reading a good book. Soon enough, a reader finds that a good book is a treasure of unlimited value: a guide, a teacher, a counselor and a friend.

PART I

SECTION 1 – The Consonants

LESSONS 1; 1.1

LESSON 1   — CONSONANTS

B b	C c = K	Cc = S	D d	F f
bone	cat	city	dog	fish
bat	cup	celery	dive	fan

Gg	Gg = J	Hh	Jj	Kk
goat	giant	house	jump	kite
gum	genie	ham	jail	kangaroo

Ll	Ll	Mm	Mm	Nn
bell	lamp	camel	mutt	pencil
melon	lion	hem	map	hen

Nn	Pp	Qq = KW		Rr
nail	panda	queen		car
nine	pupil	quail		parrot

Rr	Ss	Ss		
rat	socks	bus		
rod	six	snake		

Tt	Ww	Vv	Xx = Z	Xx = KS
toad	wagon	van	xylophone	taxi
ten	weeds	vine	xerus	fox

	Yy	Zz		
	yak	zigzag		
	yoyo	zany		

SIGHT WORDS:

we	will	use	my	van
do	you	like	to	eat
did	you	not	use	it
she	does	have	a	cat
she	likes	to	have	your cat
yes	it	has	no	fat
the	cat	eats	ate	
she	is	in	the	house

READ THE FOLLOWING SENTENCES:

The fat cat eats the fish.
Did the fat cat eat the fish?

The dog likes bones.
Does the dog like bones?

The lion jumps on the goat.
Did the lion jump on the goat?

Do we need to have a city map?
Yes, we need to have a city map.

Will you use my van?
Yes, I will use your van.

The giant panda eats weeds.
Does the giant panda eat weeds?

The pupil has a pencil.
Does the pupil have a pencil?

The goat eats the melon.
Did the goat eat the melon?

The parrot likes fish.
Does the parrot like fish?

The fox ate the hen.
Did the fox eat the hen?

The zany has no socks.
Does the zany have no socks?

The kite is not in the car.
Is the kite not in the car?

USE THE FOLLOWING WORDS IN SENTENCES:

| lamp | bell | queen | camel | pencil |
| nail | snake | taxi | giant | melon |

LESSON 1.1 — CONSONANT BLENDS AND DIGRAPHS

CONSONANT BLENDS:

bl	cl	fl	gl	pl
blaze	clover	flower	glider	plate

sl	br	cr	dr	fr
slippers	brush	crab	dragon	freezer

gr	pr	tr	sc = sk	
grape	pretzel	tree	scale	

sm	sn	sp	sq	st
smoke	snail	spoon	squirrel	steamship

	sw	cc = ks	lt	nk
	swan	accident	belt	sink

dle	gle	sk	ng	
candle	eagle	mask	wings	

ch		ph = f	sh	th
chair		telephone	shell	tooth

wh				
whale				

SIGHT WORDS:

here	there	up	and	under
the	thin	animal	comes	inside
more	clean			

READ THE FOLLOWING SENTENCES:

Can you get me the chair under the telephone?
The telephone is under the chair.

The smoke comes from the house
Do not smoke inside the house.

The squirrel is up on the tree.
Is the squirrel up on the tree?

Can I use the brush to clean the shell?
Use a clean brush on the shell.

The glider is like a kite.
Is the glider like a kite?

The animal is a giant whale.
The whale is a giant animal.

Here is spoon and a plate for you.
There is no spoon on the plate.

There is more fish in the freezer.
Is there more fish in the freezer?

USE THE FOLLOWING WORDS IN SENTENCES:

| flower | crab | slippers | knife | ghost |
| dragon | tree | clover | accident | snail |

PART I

SECTION 2 – The Vowels

LESSONS 2-6

LESSON 2

apple	egg	Indian	ox	umbrella
Aa	Ee	Ii	Oo	Uu

READ AND WRITE THE FOLLOWING WORDS:

ax	echo	igloo	odd	ugly
actor	Eskimo	ill	otter	under
add	Edna	issue	omelet	up
ago	empty	inn	on	us
after	enter	inside		utter
album	elder	it		
attic				
an				
ass				

SIGHT WORDS:

card	for	his	tree

READ THE FOLLOWING SENTENCES:

The Eskimo is inside the igloo.
Is the Eskimo inside the igloo?

Did you issue his I. D. card?
No, I did not issue his I.D. card.

The actor is ill.
Is the actor ill?

The album is for Edna.
Is the album for Edna?

The ass is under the apple tree.
The ass ate the apple under the tree.

Are the eggs for the omelet?
Yes, the eggs are for the omelet.

The attic is empty.
Is the attic empty?

Do you have an umbrella?
Yes, I have an umbrella.

USE THE FOLLOWING WORDS IN SENTENCES:

ugly	Indian	umbrella	ox	add

LESSON 3

ape	equal	ice	open	unicorn
Aa	Ee	Ii	Oo	Uu

READ AND WRITE THE FOLLOWING WORDS:

Abe	Eden	ibis	oboe	unit
ace	eleven	ivy	ode	units
ale	even	item	omit	unite
age	emu	idol	oval	use
			over	

SIGHT WORDS:

two	is	a	number	
for	sale	two	other	(units)
			more	

READ THE FOLLOWING SENTENCES:

All eggs are oval.
Are all eggs oval?

Abe, can you open the inn?
Yes, I can open the inn.

Can I use the other oboe?
Yes, you can use the other oboe.

Can the ibis get the fish?
No, the ibis can not get the fish.

Abe has an oboe
Does Abe have an oboe?

Eleven more units are up for sale.
Are eleven more units up for sale?

Two is an even number.
Is two an even number?

Eleven is an odd number.
Is eleven an odd number?

USE THE FOLLOWING WORDS IN SENTENCES:

ace	Eden	idol	unite	over

LESSON 4

tail 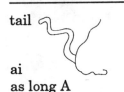   leaf   tie 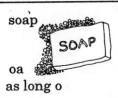   soap 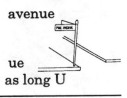   avenue

ai   ea   ie   oa   ue
as long A   as long E   as long I   as long o   as long U

READ AND WRITE THE FOLLOWING WORDS:

aid	meat	die	coat	cue
ail	easy	pie	oat	due
aim	lead	pies	boat	argue
maid	heat	lie	load	issue
nail	meal		loaf	value
pain	jeans		loan	
wait	team		soak	

SIGHT WORDS:

and	how	do	you get	into the car

READ THE FOLLOWING SENTENCES:

The ox has a tail.
Does the ox have a tail?

The maid heats the meat loaf.
Did the maid heat the meat loaf?

Can Abe wait for his other jeans?
Yes, Abe waits for his other jeans.

Abe loads a box of soap into the boat.
Did Abe load a box of soap into the boat?

Abe and the maid eat meat pies.
The maid made meat pies for Abe.

Two teams tie for the lead.
Did two teams tie for the lead?

How do you get a loan?
Is it easy to get a loan?
It is not easy to get a loan.

The tiger lies in wait for a meal.
Does the tiger lie in wait for a meal?
Wait! I will get a meal for the tiger.

USE THE FOLLOWING WORDS IN SENTENCES:

aim	soak	coat	value	team

LESSON 5

eel

ee
as long E

toe

oe
as long O

READ AND WRITE THE FOLLOWING WORDS:

beet	seed	doe
deep	tee	foe
feed	weed	hoe
heel		Joe
keep		roe
need		woe
reef		Poe

SIGHT WORDS:

you   hide   from   her

READ THE FOLLOWING SENTENCES:

The doe eats seeds and weeds.
Does the doe eat seeds and weeds?

The doe is on her feet.
Is the doe on her feet?

Two eels feed near the reef.
Do two eels feed near the reef?

Abe needs more seeds.
Does Abe need more seeds?

The other hoe is from Abe.
Is the other hoe from Abe?

Sea weeds hide the eel.
Do sea weeds hide the eel?

Roe is fish egg.
Is roe fish egg?

Joe eats roe and sea weeds.
Does Joe eat roe and sea weeds?

USE THE FOLLOWING WORDS IN SENTENCES:

heel   deep   keep   foe   beet

LESSON 6

ceiling

EI
as long E

READ AND WRITE THE FOLLOWING WORDS:

leisure   deceive
seize   either
seizure   neither
receive
receipt
deceit

SIGHT WORDS:

time   or

READ THE FOLLOWING SENTENCES:

Abe needs a receipt.   You either pay for the lamp or give it back.
Does Abe need a receipt?   I will do neither.

The otter seizes one eel.
Did the otter seize one eel?

Does Abe have more time for leisure?
Yes, Abe has more time for leisure.

Does the attic have a ceiling?
No, the attic does not have a ceiling.

USE THE FOLLOWING WORDS IN SENTENCES:

receive   deceive   seize   ceiling   leisure

PART I

SECTION 3 – Y as a Vowel

LESSONS 7-7.2

LESSON 7

baby

Y = long E

READ AND WRITE THE FOLLOWING WORDS:

lady	hefty	Billy	copy	muddy
happy	needy	hilly	foggy	pudgy
lazy	messy	dizzy	soggy	puppy
daisy	jelly	silly	holy	buddy
daddy		city	puffy	funny

READ THE FOLLOWING SENTENCES:

Billy has a puppy.
Does Billy have a puppy?

Billy's puppy is lazy.
Is Billy's puppy lazy?

Billy is happy in the city.
Is Billy happy in the city?

The daisy is like a weed.
Is the daisy like a weed?

The heat makes him dizzy.
Did the heat make him dizzy?

Can you make one more copy?
Yes, I can make one more copy.

USE THE FOLLOWING WORDS IN SENTENCES:

lady	needy	happy	muddy	jelly
silly	foggy	holy	dizzy	soggy

LESSON 7.1

spy

Y = long I

READ AND WRITE THE FOLLOWING WORDS:

by	cry	fly	dye	type
my	dry	sly	eye	hyena
rely	try	sty	rye	shy
deny	pry	sky	bye	reply

SIGHT WORDS:

too

READ THE FOLLOWING SENTENCES:

Is he too shy to reply?
Yes, he is too shy to reply.

My eye is dry.
Is my eye dry?

The spy has a keen eye.
Does the spy have a keen eye?

The hyena has an odd cry.
Does the hyena have an odd cry?

Abe, can you type a copy?
Yes, I can type a copy.

Does the ox eat rye?
Yes, the ox eats rye.

You keep an eye on Billy.
Did you keep an eye on Billy?

Did you try the dye?
No, I did not try the dye.

USE THE FOLLOWING WORDS IN SENTENCES:

sly   deny   sky   pry   rely

LESSON 7.2

cymbals

Y = short I

READ AND WRITE THE FOLLOWING WORDS:

gym	lynx	cygnet	gypsy	pygmy
symbol	system	cyst	syrup	mystery

SIGHT WORDS:

work	above		
move	the	big	swan

READ THE FOLLOWING SENTENCES:

The teams are in the gym.
Are the teams in the gym?

The gypsy is on the move.
Is the gypsy on the move?

Is the lynx a city cat?
No, the lynx is not a city cat.

The pygmy is at work.
Is the pygmy at work?

Will the system work?
No, the system will not work.

The cyst above his eye is big.
Is the cyst above his eye big?

Is the symbol a mystery?
Yes, the symbol is a mystery.

The cygnet is a baby swan.
Is the cygnet a baby swan?

USE THE FOLLOWING WORDS IN SENTENCES:

cymbals	pygmy	gym	cyst	mystery

PART I

SECTION 4 – Consonant and

Vowel Combinations

At The Beginning Of Words

LESSONS 8-35

LESSON 8

bag		bed		bib		box		bus	
ba		be		bi		bo		bu	
baby		bee		bike		boat		bugle	

READ AND WRITE THE FOLLOWING WORDS:

bake	beg	big	bog	bug
bait	beat	bite	bobbin	buzz
bad	bean	bid	boss	bud
base	Ben	bin	bon-bon	bun
bale	bet	bill		butt
back	Bess	bit		buck

EXERCISE SENTENCES:

Ben is a big baby.
Is Ben a big baby?

Ben, the baby, is in bed.
Is Ben, the baby, in bed?

A bad bedbug bites Ben.
Did a bad bedbug bite Ben?

The bib is for the baby.
Is the bib for the baby?

The box of bon-bons is not for Ben
Is the box of bon-bons for Ben?

There is a big bag of buns in the bin
Is there a big bag of buns in the bin?

Did the bees buzz by Bess?
The bees buzz by Bess.

Does Bess have a bad back?
Yes, Bess has a bad back.

USE THE FOLLOWING WORDS IN SENTENCES:

base	bet	boss	buck
bait	beat	bill	bud

LESSON 9   c = k

cat   cot   cup

ca   co   cu

cake   cone   cupid

READ AND WRITE THE FOLLOWING WORDS:

Cal	code	cut
cane	cod	cute
cap	cop	Cuba
cab	cob	cub
cage	cock	cube
cave		

SIGHT WORDS:

there   are   some   cupcakes

READ THE FOLLOWING SENTENCES:

Bess bakes some more cupcakes.   Will Cal use the cot?
Did Bess bake some more cupcakes?   Yes, Cal will use the cot.

The cub in the cage is cute.   The eel is inside the cove.
Is the cub in the cage cute.   Is the eel inside the cove?

Two big cats are in the cave.   There are ice cubes in the cup.
Are there two big cats in the cave?   Are there ice cubes in the cup?

Did Bess cut the cake?   Abe did not get his coat back.
Yes, Bess cut the cake.   Did Abe get his coat back?

USE THE FOLLOWING WORDS IN SENTENCES:

cut	cap	cane	cod	Cuba
cab	cupid	cob	cage	cake

LESSON 10 c = s

cent	city	cymbals
ce	ci	cy
cedar	cider	cyclone

READ AND WRITE THE FOLLOWING WORDS:

cellar   cinema
ceiling   cinder
celery   citizen
cell   cinder
cease

SIGHT WORDS:

yet

READ THE FOLLOWING SENTENCES:

The cinder box is in the bin.
Is the cinder box in the bin?

The other cup of cider is for Cal.
Is the other cup of cider for Cal?

The celery is for eleven cents.
Is the celery for eleven cents?

Does the attic need a ceiling?
Yes, the attic needs a ceiling.

The cells are empty.
Are the cells empty?

Is Cal a city cop?
Yes, Cal is a city cop.

Is the cinema open?
Yes, the cinema is open.

He is not a citizen yet.
Is he not a citizen, yet?

USE THE FOLLOWING WORDS IN SENTENCES:

cellar   cease   citizen   cedar   cider

LESSON 11

daddy		den		dill		doll		duck	
da		de		di		do		du	
daisy		deep		dine		doe		duke	

READ AND WRITE THE FOLLOWING WORDS:

Dane	deal	dig	Don	dune
dash	deck	dice	dock	duty
daze	deem	dim	dome	dummy
date	dell	dip	doze	dull
dame	dear	dime	dose	dub
dam		discus	dole	dud

READ THE FOLLOWING SENTENCES:

The ax is dull.
Is the ax dull?

Is the dame in the cab Don's date?
The dame in the cab is Don's date.

The dill is for a dime.
Is the dill for a dime?

The doll is cute.
Is the doll cute?

Don dines in the den.
Does Don dine in the den?

Big Bill is a Dane.
Is big Bill a Dane?

Bill is on duty.
Is Bill on duty?

The sea is deep over there.
Is the sea deep over there?

USE THE FOLLOWING WORDS IN SENTENCES:

dam	dash	dice	dock	dull
deck	dose	dummy	deal	duck

LESSON 12

fan		fence		fish		fox		funnel
fa		fe		fi		fo		fu
face		feet		five		foal		fuse

READ AND WRITE THE FOLLOWING WORDS:

fame	fed	Fido	foam	fume
fad	feel	fins	fodder	fumes
fade	fell	fine	fog	fuel
fancy	fear	fill	focus	fun
fate	fee	fit		fuss
fail	feat			

SIGHT WORDS:

last   forever

READ THE FOLLOWING SENTENCES:

Can you focus on the fan's face?
Yes, I can focus on the fan's face

Does fame last forever?
No, fame does not last forever.

Was it fun to feed Fido?
It was fun to feed Fido!

The fox ate the fat duck.
Did the fox eat the fat duck?

The fumes made Bess ill.
Did the fumes make Bess ill?

Fish have fins.
Do fish have fins?

There is no fuel on the bus.
Is there fuel on the bus?

The jeans are a fine fit for Billy.
Are the jeans a fine fit for Billy?

USE THE FOLLOWING WORDS IN SENTENCES:

fail	feel	fill	foam	fuel
fancy	fee	fuss	fade	fence

LESSON 13

gal	bagel	gift	golf	gum
ga	ge	gi	go	gu
gate	geese		goat	legume

READ AND WRITE THE FOLLOWING WORDS:

gave	get	gill	got	gut
Gabby		gibbon	goad	guppy
gas		giddy	goal	gull
game			god	gun
gag			goby	gush
gander				Gus

SIGHT WORDS:

much   mental   chess

READ THE FOLLOWING SENTENCES:

The gull gags on the goby.   Fish have fins and gills.
Did the gull gag on the goby?   Do fish have fins and gills?

Do geese eat weeds as much as goats?   Is the guppy a fish?
Yes, geese eat weeds as much as goats do?   Yes, the guppy is a fish.

The gal by the gate has a bagel.   Does the guppy have fins and gills?
Does the gal by the gate have a bagel?   Yes, the guppy has fins and gills.

Gabby got Gus a fine gander.   Chess is a mental game.
Gabby, did you get Gus a fine gander?   Is chess a mental game?

USE THE FOLLOWING WORDS IN SENTENCES:

gas   goal   game   gun   gander

LESSON 14   g = j

gem	ginger	gymnast
ge	gi	gy = gi
genie	giant	

READ AND WRITE THE FOLLOWING WORDS:

gadget	giblet	gyp
Gene	gin	gypsy
gel	gibber	
budget	gibbet	
fidget		

SIGHT WORDS:

good	now	taste	this
this	is	a	mess

READ THE FOLLOWING SENTENCES:

Are there genies and giants?
No, there are no genies and giants.

The other gadget is in the gym.
Is the other gadget in the gym?
The other gym has no gadget like this.

The gin and ginger ale made her giddy.
Did the gin and ginger ale make her giddy?

Does Gene use the gadget in the gym?
Yes, Gene uses the gadget in the gym.

There is no use for the gibbet now.
Is there use for the gibbet now?

The giblet tastes good.
Does the giblet taste good?
Good, you taste the giblet.

The budget is a mess.
Is the budget a mess?

Gene uses gel.
Does Gene use gel?

USE THE FOLLOWING WORDS IN SENTENCES:

gymnast	gem	ginger	gypsy	gel

LESSON 15

hat		hen		hill		hog		hut	
ha		he		hi		ho		hu	
halo		hero		hive		hose		human	

READ AND WRITE THE FOLLOWING WORDS:

hack	heal	hiccup	hobby	hub
hate	heap	him	home	hum
hag	heed	hip	hotel	hug
haze	hell	hiss	hole	hull
Hal	heave	hide	hot	huge

SIGHT WORDS:

give   hamburger   and   coffee

READ THE FOLLOWING SENTENCES:

The hose has a huge hole.
Does the hose have a huge hole?

Hal gave Bess a big hug.
Did Hal give Bess a big hug?

Bob has a hobby.
Does Bob have a hobby?

Bob had a hamburger and two cups of coffee.
Did Bob have a hamburger
    and two cups of coffee?

Bob heaves the discus.
Did Bob heave the discus?

Hal is happy to be home.
Is Hal happy to be home?

The hen hides from the fox.
Does the hen hide from the fox?

Did Hal and Bess eat ham and eggs?
Hal and Bess ate ham and eggs.

USE THE FOLLOWING WORDS IN SENTENCES:

hiccup	heal	heap	hole	hum
hip	hot	hog	hush	hotel

Lesson 16

jacket		jet		jigsaw		jockey		jug	
ja		je		ji		jo		ju	
jail		jeep		jibe		joker		judo	

READ AND WRITE THE FOLLOWING WORDS:

jab	jeans	jingle	job	jumbo
jam	Jenny	jig	jog	July
jade	jelly	jib	Jody	June
Jane	jeer	Jim	jot	jut
Jake			jolly	jute
jazz			joke	just

SIGHT WORDS:

new   hangar

EXERCISE SENTENCES

Jumbo jets jam the hangar.
Do jumbo jets jam the hangar?

Are jelly beans in the jute bag?
Yes, the jelly beans are in the jute bag.

Jam and jelly are all over his jeans.
Are jam and jelly all over his jeans?

His job is to cut jade and other gems.
Is his job to cut jade and other gems?

Jody jogs daily.
Does Jody jog daily?

The boat needs a new jib.
Does the boat need a new jib?

Do you like jazz?
Yes, I like jazz.

Is there cider in the jug?
Yes, there is cider in the jug.

USE THE FOLLOWING WORDS IN SENTENCES:

jab	jam	joke	jelly	just

LESSON 17

kangaroo   kennel   kitten

ka   ke   ki   ko

kale   keel   kite   koala

READ AND WRITE THE FOLLOWING WORDS:

kapok tree	keen	kin	Kodiak bear
Kate	keep	kit	kola nut
	ken	kiss	
	keg	king	
	keno	kid	
		kick	
		kill	

SIGHT WORDS:

love   cabbage

READ THE FOLLOWING SENTENCES:

Kale is a cabbage.

Is kale a cabbage?

The boat keels over.

Did the boat keel over?

Keep the kids from the kitten.

Yes, I will keep the kids from the kitten.

The kids will keep the kitten.

Will the kids keep the kitten?

The king keeps a keen eye on his kin.

Does the king keep a keen eye on his kin?

Kids love to fly kites.

Do kids love to fly kites?

Don, you kiss Kate bye-bye.

Don, did you kiss Kate bye-bye?

The keg is empty.

Is the keg empty?

USE THE FOLLOWING WORDS IN SENTENCES:

kangaroo   kennel   Kodiak bear   kick   keen

LESSON 18

lamp	lemon	lizard	lobster	lumber
la	le	li	lo	lu
lace	leaf	lion	locust	lute

READ AND WRITE THE FOLLOWING WORDS:

lap	leak	lick	lock	luck
lake	lead	live	load	Luke
lady	let	lit	log	lug
lad	leg	lid	loan	lull
late	lean	line	lob	lullaby
lane	leave	lip	lot	

READ THE FOLLOWING SENTENCES:

There is a line of cabs in this lane.
Is there a line of cabs in this lane?

Luke likes to bike by the lake.
Does Luke like to bike by the lake?

You let Luke get a lid for the jug.
Did you let Luke get a lid for the jug?

The lad's legs are lean.
Are the lad's legs lean?

Does Luke like to leave now?
Yes, Luke likes to leave now.

The lady jogs by the lake.
Does the lady jog by the lake?

Can Luke apply for a loan?
Yes, Luke can apply for a loan.

There is a leak in the dam.
Is there a leak in the dam?

USE THE FOLLOWING WORDS IN SENTENCES:

lamp	lace	lemon	leaf	lumber
lion	lullaby	luck	lick	lock

LESSON 19

map	medic	mitt	mop	mutt
ma	me	mi	mo	mu
mail	meter	mice	motor	music

READ AND WRITE THE FOLLOWING WORDS:

mad	medal	Midas	model	mud
mane	met	mite	moss	mug
mailman	meet	mile	mole	mule
maze	men	miss	motel	mummy
mate	mean	mine	moan	muff
mat				mute

SIGHT WORDS:

who	won	after

READ THE FOLLOWING SENTENCES:

Do not miss your meal!
Did you miss your meal?

The mutt made a mess of the mat.
Did the mutt make a mess of the mat?

The man and the mule fell into the mud.
The man and the mule fell into the mud.

The model has a mole on her face.
Does the model have a mole on her face?

The mailman is in the motel.
Is the mailman in the motel?

The men will meet at the motel.
Will the men meet at the motel?

Don had a melon after his meal.
Don had a melon for his meal.

Who won a medal in the mile race?
Jody won a medal in the mile race.

USE THE FOLLOWING WORDS IN SENTENCES:

mean	mine	mug	mad	mane
mat	mop	mule	mute	music

LESSON 20

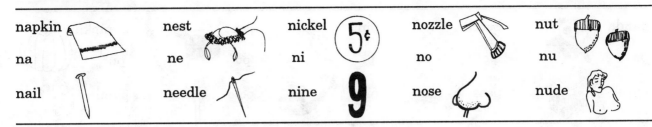

napkin	nest	nickel 5¢	nozzle	nut
na	ne	ni	no	nu
nail	needle	nine 9	nose	nude

READ AND WRITE THE FOLLOWING WORDS:

nag	neck	nip	egg nog	nugget
nape	negate	nil	nomad	nun
name	near	nice	note	nutmeg
Nate	net	nick	nod	
nanny	neat		nominee	
navy	never			

SIGHT WORDS:

Oscar	takes	care	of	coconut

READ THE FOLLOWING SENTENCES:

The nanny takes care of the baby.
Does the nanny take care of the baby?

Does a cat have nine lives?
No, a cat does not have nine lives.

The Oscar nominee is a fine actor.
Is the Oscar nominee a fine actor?

More nuns care for the needy.
Do more nuns care for the needy?

Does the coconut have a number of uses?
Yes, the coconut has a number of uses.

Did Cal nip Nate's nape?
Yes, Cal nipped Nate's nape.

The nomad, like the gypsy, is ever on the move.
Ever on the move, the nomad is like the gypsy.

The house on the hill is nice and neat.
It is nice to have a house on the hill.

USE THE FOLLOWING WORDS IN SENTENCES:

navy	name	never	nod	nugget
nose	nickle	nest	napkin	nail

LESSON 21

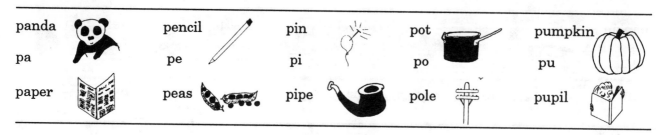

panda	pencil	pin	pot	pumpkin
pa	pe	pi	po	pu
paper	peas	pipe	pole	pupil

READ AND WRITE THE FOLLOWING WORDS:

pack	peak	pick	pollen	pub
Pam	peel	pill	poke	puppet
pad	peg	pipe	pod	puny
pave	peep	pin	pope	pug
pans	pet	pine	pop	puck
pane	pepper	pig		

SIGHT WORDS:

backpack   banana

READ THE FOLLOWING SENTENCES:

Do pupils need paper and pencil?
Yes, pupils need paper and pencil.

Can you pat or pet the panda in the cage?
No, do not pat or pet the panda in the cage.

The pig in the pigpen eats banana peels.
Does the pig in the pigpen eat banana peels?

Did you get the pot and pan from Pam?
Yes, I got the pot and pan from Pam.

The meat pie has peas and pepper.
Does the meat pie have peas and pepper?

The pupil picks up his backpack.
Did the pupil pick up his backpack?

The mass is for the pope.
Is the mass for the pope?

The pipe fits into the hole.
Does the pipe fit into the hole?

USE THE FOLLOWING WORDS IN SENTENCES:

pad	peg	pill	pole	panda
paper	pupil	pumpkin	pole	pin

LESSON 22   qu = kw

quagmire	question mark	quilt	quonset hut
qua	que	qui	quo
quail	queen	quiet	quotation mark " "

READ AND WRITE THE FOLLOWING WORDS:

quake	request	quiz	quota
quack	queer	quick	quote
quaver	query	quicker	
		quite	
		quip	
		quit	

SIGHT WORDS:

eagle   strike   struck   than   morning

READ THE FOLLOWING SENTENCES:

The eagle was quicker than the quail.   The quiz was quite easy.
Was the eagle quicker than the quail?   Was the quiz quite easy?

The music is for a quintet.   Is it hot inside the quonset hut?
Is the music for a quintet?   It is quite hot inside the quonset hut.

He quit the race after a mile.   Each man will get a quota of pills.
Did he quit the race after a mile?   Will each man get a quota of pills?

Does the queen like quail eggs?   The quake struck at two in the morning.
Yes, the queen likes quail eggs.   Did the quake strike at two in the morning?

USE THE FOLLOWING WORDS IN SENTENCES:

quilt   request   queer   quip   question

LESSON 23

QU = **K** as in mosquito

READ AND WRITE THE FOLLOWING WORDS:

antique   etiquette   Monique   mosque   liquor
                 conquer   mannequin   unique
                                                                      lacquer

SIGHT WORD:

life-like

READ THE FOLLOWING SENTENCES:

Do you need a mosquito net for the baby?   Is liquor sale up?
Yes, I need a mosquito net for the baby.   Yes, liquor sale is up.

The kangaroo is a unique animal.   The bed is an antique.
Is the kangaroo a unique animal?   Is the bed an antique?

The mosque is quiet at this time.   The mannequin is life-like.
Is the mosque quiet at this time?   Is the mannequin life-like?

The mosque is a Moslem holy house.

USE THE FOLLOWING WORDS IN SENTENCES:

conquer   etiquette   unique   antique

LESSON 24

rabbit		record		ring		rod		rug	
ra		re		ri		ro		ru	
rain		read		rice		robe			

READ AND WRITE THE FOLLOWING WORDS:

raise	recap	ribbon	robin	rub
race	reap	ripe	Rob	rubber
raider	reel	rib	role	rudder
rap	referee	rip	rope	run
ran	reed	ride	rot	rush
rat	red	rid	rose	rum

READ THE FOLLOWING SENTENCES:

Rob will run the mile race.
Will Rob run the mile race?

Red Rose is an Indian lady.
The Indian gave the lady a red rose.

Robbie does not like his role as referee.
Does Robbie like his role as referee?

Red robins ate the rice.
Did the red robins eat the rice?

Rob got rid of his other rod and reel.
Did Rob get rid of his other rod and reel?

Will the rope rot under the rain?
Yes, the rope will rot under the rain.

There was a mad rush to the rides.
Was there a mad rush to the rides?

The rabbit and the rat ran a race.
Did the rabbit and the rat run a race?

USE THE FOLLOWING WORDS IN SENTENCES:

read	record	ring	robe	rubber
raise	reed	ripe		

LESSON 25

READ AND WRITE THE FOLLOWING WORDS:

arrow	error	irate	ore	Uranus
arrive	era	irrigate	organ	urn
arise	erode	iris	orbit	urinal
armor	erase	iron	order	
army		irritate	orange	

SIGHT WORDS:

end	useless	zeal
thin	indeed	

READ THE FOLLOWING SENTENCES:

His armor is thin and useless.
Is his armor thin and useless?

Uranus orbits the sun.
Does Uranus orbit the sun?

His order of oranges arrives late.
Did his order of oranges arrive late?
Did you order a box of oranges?

Arrows rain upon the army.
Did arrows rain upon the army?

His zeal led to error.
Did his zeal lead to error?

Irate fans are by the iron gate.
Are irate fans by the iron gate?

There is iron ore in the mine.
Is there an iron ore in the mine?
The iron ore is mine.

Is it the end of an era?
Indeed, it is the end of an era.

USE THE FOLLOWING WORDS IN SENTENCES:

arrive	erase	irritate	organ	urinal

LESSON 26

READ AND WRITE THE FOLLOWING WORDS:

beggar	beer	fire	bore	burr
car	seer	lyre	tore	burden
fare	peer	wire	fore	quarter
hair	hear	sir	wore	fur
garden	rear	hire	pore	purr
pair		tire	sore	nurse

SIGHT WORD:
airfare

READ THE FOLLOWING SENTENCES:

Abe, can you wire the ceiling?
Yes, I can wire the ceiling.

Do you hear the cat purr?
Yes, I hear the cat purr.

The beggar needs a lot of care.
Does the beggar need a lot of care?

Don, you get a pair of tires for the car.
Don, did you get a pair of tires for the car?

Bess has a red ribbon in her hair.
Does Bess have a red ribbon in her hair?

All deer fear fire.
I fear the fire will kill the deer.

Airlines will raise airfare this June.
Will airlines raise airfare this June?

USE THE FOLLOWING WORDS IN SENTENCES:

fare	garden	sore	burden	wire

LESSON 27

Santa		seven	7	sink		socks		sun	
sa		se		si		so		su	
saber		seal		sideline		soda		suture	

READ AND WRITE THE FOLLOWING WORDS:

Sally	seep	sin	sob	submit
sack	season	sill	soak	suck
sat	set	sip	sofa	supper
safe	seek	sit	son	sullen
sale	sell	size	sole	summer

SIGHT WORDS:

buys	buy	art	work
clogged	now		

READ THE FOLLOWING SENTENCES:

He buys and sells in the dry season.
Does he buy and sell in the dry season?

His son sips soda.
Does his son sip soda?

He had sole and beans for supper.
Did he have sole and beans for supper?

Sally sat by the sill with her doll.
Did Sally sit by the sill with her doll?

The sun sets late in the summer.
Does the sun set late in the summer?

Sally will submit her art work now.
Will Sally submit her art work now?

He buys a safe at the sale.
Did he buy a safe at the sale?

The boat sinks into the sea.
The sink hole is clogged.

USE THE FOLLOWING WORDS IN SENTENCES:

sack	seat	sick	sofa	socks
suck	seal	saber	sideline	suture

LESSON 28

S = Z as in fuse

READ AND WRITE THE FOLLOWING WORDS:

abuse	accuse	amuse	his	fuse
ruse	alms	reason	runs	as
hers	goes	does	buds	hugs
use				

S = SH as in sugar

READ AND WRITE THE FOLLOWING WORDS:

censure	sure	assure	ensure	fissure
insure	sugary	sugarless	sureness	surety

SIGHT WORDS:

one	anyone	well

READ THE FOLLOWING SENTENCES:

Does sugar have many uses?
Yes, sugar has many uses.

Sally runs daily to keep fit.
Does Sally run daily to keep fit?

His antics amuse no one.
Do his antics amuse anyone?

Sugarless gums sell well.
Do sugarless gums sell well?

There is no sure cure for AIDS.
Is there a sure cure for AIDS?

Did you insure your car?
Yes, I did insure my car.

USE THE FOLLOWING WORDS IN SENTENCES:

accuse	alms	buds
censure	hugs	fissure

LESSON 29

tablet		telephone		tin		top		tub	
ta		te		ti		to		tu	
table		tepee		tile		token		tulip	

READ AND WRITE THE FOLLOWING WORDS:

tape	teeter	tide	tot	tutor
tap	tease	tidy	tote	tuna
tan	temper	time	toddy	tug
tame	teem	timber	tomcat	tugboat
take	teak	tipsy	tomato	tumor
tadpole	teddy bear	tin	ton	tune

SIGHT WORDS:

him	timberline	becomes	finals
wood	cabinets		

READ THE FOLLOWING SENTENCES:

Tons of tin cans litter the timberline.
Do tons of tin cans litter the timberline?

The top ten teams enter the finals.
Do the top ten teams enter the finals?

Tigers have mean tempers.
Do tigers have mean tempers?

It is time to take the tomcat back in.
Is it time to take the tomcat back in.

The toddy made him tipsy.
Did the toddy make him tipsy?

The lake teems with tiny tadpoles.
Does the lake teem with tiny tadpoles?

The tadpole becomes a toad.
Does the tadpole become a toad?

Teak wood makes fine cabinets.
Does teak wood make fine cabinets?

USE THE FOLLOWING WORDS IN SENTENCES:

telephone	table	tulip	tepee	tutor
tease	tap	token	tile	tub

LESSON 30

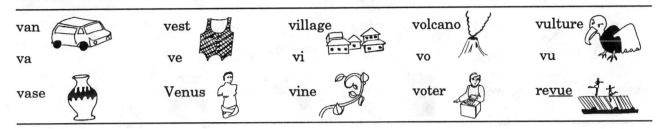

van	vest	village	volcano	vulture
va	ve	vi	vo	vu
vase	Venus	vine	voter	revue

READ AND WRITE THE FOLLOWING WORDS:

valentine	velvet	villa	vodka	vulgar
vacate	veal	vigor	vocal	
vandal	vessel	visitor	vote	
vampire	venom	viper	vomit	
vane	vendor	vitamin		
vat		vim		

READ THE FOLLOWING SENTENCES:

Will voters vote on the tax raise?
The voters will vote on the tax raise.

You need meat for vim and vigor.
Do you need meat for vim and vigor?

Will you be my valentine?
Sure, I will be your valentine.

Vipers have a lot of venom.
Do vipers have a lot of venom?

Visitors use a van to go to the hill top villa.
Do visitors use a van to go to the hill top villa?

There are vampire bats, but no vampires.
Are there vampire bats, but no vampires?

Hal gave Bess her vitamin pill.
Did Hal give Bess her vitamin pill?

He seasons veal with pepper.
Does he season veal with pepper?

USE THE FOLLOWING WORDS IN SENTENCES:

vest	volcano	vulture	vodka	vulgar
vase	Venus	vine	vandal	vomit

LESSON 31

wagon		web		wings		wobble	
wa		we		wi		wo	
wave		weave		wipe		woe	

READ AND WRITE THE FOLLOWING WORDS:

wag	weak	win	wok
wage	wed	wine	woke
wad	welcome	wigwam	wonder
wade	weasel	witness	won
wax	wet	wide	wove
wash	weep	wives	

SIGHT WORDS:

cover	story
group	area

READ THE FOLLOWING SENTENCES:

The witness wove a weak story.
Did the witness weave a weak story?

The weasel feeds on rats and mice.
Does the weasel feed on rats and mice?

A group of wives will welcome visitors.
Will a group of wives welcome visitors?

Don, will you wipe and wax the car?
Yes, I will wipe and wax the car.

Weeds cover a wide area of the garden.
Do weeds cover a wide area of the garden?

You wipe your wet feet, Don.
Don, did you wipe your wet feet?

The wigwam is an Indian hut.
Is the wigwam an Indian hut?

Is there wine in the cellar?
The wine cellar is empty.

USE THE FOLLOWING WORDS IN SENTENCES:

wage	wonder	weep	wagon	win
wade	web	wings	wobble	wok

LESSON 32 X = Z

xa   xe   xi   xu
Xavier   xerus   xylophone   luxury
                                                liner

READ AND WRITE THE FOLLOWING WORDS:
Xavier   xebec   xylem
                xenon

SIGHT WORDS:
what   African   ground
doing   sailing
woody   part

EXERCISE SENTENCES:
The xebec has sails.   Is xenon a gas?
Does the xebec have sails?   Yes, xenon is a gas.

The xylophone makes fine music.   The luxury liner is at sea.
Does the xylophone make fine music? Sailing at sea is a luxury.

Is the xerus an African ground squirrel?   What is xylem?
Yes, the xerus is an African ground squirrel. Xylem is the woody part of a tree.

Is Xavier doing art work now?
Yes, Xavier is doing art work now.

LESSON 33

X = KS as in six

READ AND WRITE THE FOLLOWING WORDS:

addax	Texan	fix	boxer	tuxedo
ax	excuse	mixer	hoax	buxom
Max	Mexican	mix	box	
relax	exercise	vixen		
tax	exceed			
	excite			

SIGHT WORDS:

female   limit

READ THE FOLLOWING SENTENCES:

A tuxedo is a luxury for him.

Is a tuxedo a luxury for him?

There is a tax on luxury items.

Is there a tax on luxury items?

The boxers relax inside the gym.

Do the boxers relax inside the gym?

The napkins are in the box.

Are the napkins in the box?

Jody jogs to exercise.

Does Jody jog to exercise?

Is the vixen a female fox?

The vixen is a female fox.

Can I exceed the limit of six doses?

No, do not exceed the limit of six doses.

USE THE FOLLOWING WORDS IN SENTENCES:

excuse   exercise   relax   mix   tuxedo

LESSON 33.1

X = GZ as in exit

READ AND WRITE THE FOLLOWING WORDS:

examine   exempt   exile   exotic
exact   exhibit

SIGHT WORD:

enough

READ THE FOLLOWING SENTENCES:

The exile leads a nomad's life.
Does the exile lead a nomad's life?

There is an exhibit of exotic sea life.
Is there an exhibit of exotic sea life?

Are the exits wide enough?
Many exits are not wide enough.

Some sales are tax exempt.
Are some sales tax exempt?

The tuxedo is an exact fit for him.
Is the tuxedo an exact fit for him?

USE THE FOLLOWING WORDS IN SENTENCES:

exile   exempt   exhibit   examine   exotic

LESSON 34

yak	yellow	yip	yonder	yucca
ya	ye	yi	yo	yu
	yeast	yipe	yoyo	Yule

READ AND WRITE THE FOLLOWING WORDS:

yam	yell	yipee	yodel
yap	yet		yoke
ban<u>yan</u>	yes		yogi
	yen		yoga
	year		yokel
	yearly		can<u>yon</u>

SIGHT WORDS:

tilling   soil
put

READ THE FOLLOWING SENTENCES:

You put a yoke on the yak.
Did you put a yoke on the yak?

Did he get a yoyo for his son, yet?
Yes, he got a yoyo for his son.

Yule is a happy season.
Is Yule a happy season?

The yogi sits on a yellow mat.
Does the yogi sit on a yellow mat?

Over yonder is the river.
Is the river over yonder?

He yells, "Yipe!"
Did he yell, "Yipe"?

The yokel is tilling the soil.
Is the yokel tilling the soil?

Is it hard to yodel?
Not all can do a yodel.

USE THE FOLLOWING WORDS IN SENTENCES:

yucca   year   yearly   yeast   banyan

LESSON 35

zap	zeppelin	zipper	zombie	
za	ze	zi	zo	Z = TS
zany	zebra		zone	pizza

READ AND WRITE THE FOLLOWING WORDS:

zax	zero	zigzag	zodiac
Zanzibar	zebu	zippy	
Zambesi	zeal	zip	

Z = TS

Nazi	pizzeria	quartz	waltz

SIGHT WORDS:

Africa	river	military	antics	until

READ THE FOLLOWING SENTENCES:

The zebu and the yak are big animals.
Are the zebu and the yak big animals?

He got a zero on the exam.
Did he get a zero on the exam?

Zanzibar is in Africa.
Is Zanzibar in Africa?

Zambesi is a river in Africa.
Is Zambesi a river in Africa?

The zigzag road makes him dizzy.
Did the zigzag road make him dizzy?
The road zigzags to the top of the hill.

Kids love zany antics.
Do kids love zany antics?
The zany amuses the kids with his antics.

The zeppelin is over the military zone.
Is the zeppelin over the military zone?

The pizzeria is open until ten.
Is the pizzeria open until ten?

USE THE FOLLOWING WORDS IN SENTENCES:

pizza	zombie	zebra	zipper	zeppelin

PART I

SECTION 5 – Other Combinations

Producing Long And

Short Vowel Sounds

LESSONS 36-38

LESSON 36

hay	key	buy	arrow	dew
AY = long A	EY = long E	UY & AY = long I	OW = long O	EW= long U

READ AND WRITE THE FOLLOWING WORDS:

bay	donkey	buy	elbow	few
decay	monkey	kayak	window	curfew
day	barley	guy	bowl	new
away	honey		undertow	pew
payday	valley		low	mildew
ray	kidney		below	view
say	money		narrow	review

SIGHT WORD:

canoe

READ THE FOLLOWING SENTENCES:

Pay day is five days away.
Is pay day five days away?

The bale of hay is for the donkey.
Is the bale of hay for the donkey?

Sam buys barley and honey in the valley.
Does Sam buy barley and honey in the valley?

Is the kayak an Eskimo's canoe?
Yes, the kayak is an Eskimo's canoe.

The guys are on the way to the bay.
Are the guys on the way to the bay?

Tom will fix the bay window.
Will Tom fix the bay window?

The back row needs a new pew.
Does the back row need a new pew?

Here is a nice view of the valley.
Is this a nice view of the valley?

USE THE FOLLOWING WORDS IN SENTENCES:

decay	key	dew	away	elbow
kidney	bowl	money	mildew	curfew

LESSON 37

eight	prey	field	guide	eunuch
EI = long A	EY = long A	IE = long E	UI = long I	EU = long U CH = K

READ AND WRITE THE FOLLOWING WORDS:

lei	hey	belief	guide	Europe
reign	survey	believe	guise	Eurasia
neigh	convey	diesel	disguise	neutral
neighbor	obey	niece	guile	feud
weigh		relief	beguile	
weight		relieve		
vein		piece		
veils				

READ THE FOLLOWING SENTENCES:

Use the survey as your guide to action.
As a guide to action, use the survey.

Tom lost weight due to his illness.
Did Tom lose weight due to his illness?

His neighbor has a pet monkey.
Does his neighbor have a pet monkey?

The reign of terror is over for some men.
Is the reign of terror over for some men?

Fog veils the valley from view.
Does fog veil the valley from view?

Welcome leis are given to visitors.
Are welcome leis given to visitors?

The madman is a devil in disguise.
Is the madman a devil in disguise?

The tiger waits for a prey.
Does the tiger wait for a prey?

USE THE FOLLOWING WORDS IN SENTENCES:

vein	rein	field	niece	piece
feud	neutral	obey	diesel	believe

LESSON 38

laugh	bread	guitar	cough	couple
AU = short A GH = F	EA, EO as short E	U, UI as short I	OU = short O GH = F	OU = short U GH = F

READ AND WRITE THE FOLLOWING WORDS:

laugh	dead	biscuit	cough	rough
aunt	weapon	busy		roughen
	read	business		double
	ahead	build		tough
	meadow	built		toughen
	lead	guilt		touch
	heaven			enough
	heavy			
	leopard			
	guess			

READ THE FOLLOWING SENTENCES:

Abe has a loaf of bread.
Does Abe have a loaf of bread?

The reefs are dead ahead.
Are the reefs dead ahead?

Abe's cough is bad.
Is Abe's cough bad?

The man is in the biscuit business.
Is the man in the biscuit business?

Lead is a heavy metal.
Is lead a heavy metal?

The cow is in the meadow.
Is the cow in the meadow?

Has Peter read the book *Heaven Can Wait*?
Yes, Peter has read the book, *Heaven Can Wait*.

The bow and arrow is a weapon.
Is the bow and arrow a weapon?

USE THE FOLLOWING WORDS IN SENTENCES:

laugh	guitar	leopard	biscuit	busy
ahead	guess	rough	build	double

PART I

SECTION 6 – The Half O Sound

LESSON 39

LESSON 39

wall

AL

faucet

AU
as half O

paw

AW

READ AND WRITE THE FOLLOWING WORDS:

all	always	auk	pause	awe	saw
call	also	auto	Paul	awl	raw
tall	balk	autumn	haul	pawn	law
walk	talk	maul	cause	bawl	jaw
altar	mall	gauze	because	yawn	lawn

SIGHT WORDS:

good   colorful

READ THE FOLLOWING SENTENCES:

Are all laws good?
No, not all laws are good.

He pauses by the auto.
Did he pause by the auto?

The cat's paw is raw.
Is the cat's paw raw?

The tiger mauls the deer.
Did the tiger maul the deer?

Tom walks to exercise.
Does Tom walk to exercise?

The auk dives into the sea.
Did the auk dive into the sea?

Autumn is a colorful season.
Is autumn a colorful season?

Can you fix the faucet on the lawn?
Yes, I can fix the faucet on the lawn.

USE THE FOLLOWING WORDS IN SENTENCES:

faucet	wall	pauper	altar	tall
cause	pause	jaw	always	pawn

PART I

SECTION 7 – The Double O Sounds

LESSONS 40-41

LESSON 40

moose

long OO

book

short OO

READ AND WRITE THE FOLLOWING WORDS:

boot	fool	cook	wood
moon	goose	foot	wool
roof	coop	good	hoof
food	room	hook	hood
boo	noose	look	poor
hoot	pool	nook	soot
bamboo			

READ THE FOLLOWING SENTENCES:

The maid cooks good food.
Does the maid cook good food?

The doctor takes a good look at Dan's foot.
Did the doctor take a good look at Dan's foot?

The goose is in the coop.
Is the goose in the coop?

Fans hoot and boo the actors.
Did fans hoot and boo the actors?

The coop is made of bamboo and wood.
Is the coop made of bamboo and wood?

The roof over his room has a leak.
Does the roof over his room leak?

Is the eel off the hook?
Yes, the eel is off the hook.

Are the books in the room?
The books are in the room.

USE THE FOLLOWING WORDS IN SENTENCES:

boot	moose	moon	poor	cook
soot	food	pool	good	goose

LESSON 41

juice   movie   jewel   toucan   wolf

U, UE, UI = long OO   O = long O   EW = long OO   OU = long OO   O = short OO

READ AND WRITE THE FOLLOWING WORDS:

tuna	movie	Jew	nougat	wolf
suit	loser	jewel	cougar	wolves
bruin	do	sewage	ghoul	woman
glue	doer	sewer	mousse	
true	to	brew	route	
bruise	today	chew	soup	
fruit	tomorrow	flew	roulette	
ruby	move		coupon	
super				

READ THE FOLLOWING SENTENCES:

All the fruits have bruises.
Do all the fruits have bruises?

Glue is very useful.
Is glue very useful?

True ruby is a rare jewel.
Is true ruby a rare jewel?

Tuna is a game fish.
Is tuna a game fish?

Sam needs mousse for his hair.
Does Sam need mousse for his hair?

A very bad move made him lose the game.
Did he lose the game because of
   a very bad move?

The movie "Jewel of the Nile"
   made a lot of money.
Did the movie "Jewel of the Nile"
   make a lot of money?

There is hot soup in the pot.
Is there hot soup in the pot?

The toucan has a big beak.
Does the toucan have a big beak?

Route Eleven is an easy route.
Is Route Eleven an easy route?

USE THE FOLLOWING WORDS IN SENTENCES:

juice	movie	today	jewel	wolf
useful	doer	chew	coupon	woman

PART I

SECTION 8 – The Diphthongs

LESSONS 42-43

LESSON 42

coin   oyster

OI   OY

READ AND WRITE THE FOLLOWING WORDS:

oil	poison	boy	Doyle
voice	rejoin	alloy	convoy
loiter	noise	toy	annoy
foil	poise	enjoy	ahoy
avoid	boil	decoy	

READ THE FOLLOWING SENTENCES:

The boy's toys are also inside the box.
Are the boy's toys also inside the box?

Is the voice of reason always loud enough to hear?
No, the voice of reason is not
      always loud enough to hear.

Ducks made of wood are used as decoys.
Are ducks made of wood used as decoys?

Will you boil water for the oysters?
Yes, I will boil water for the oysters.

A copper alloy is used to make coins.
Are coins made out of a copper alloy?

Sam enjoys the oysters.
Does Sam enjoy the oysters?

The maid avoids the use of animal oil.
Does the maid avoid the use of animal oil?

Will Doyle rejoin the convoy now?
No, Doyle will rejoin the convoy tomorrow.

USE THE FOLLOWING WORDS IN SENTENCES;

coin   poison   annoy   loiter   ahoy

LESSON 43

house
OU

cow
OW

READ AND WRITE THE FOLLOWING WORDS:

out	mouse	allow	tower
bout	mouth	how	towel
pout	joust	down	gown
foul	oust	now	town
loud	south	vow	owl
douse	rout	rowdy	howl

SIGHT WORDS:

through   again

READ THE FOLLOWING SENTENCES:

The sow is inside the pigpen.
Is the sow inside the pigpen?

How did the mouse get into the house?
The mouse in the house got in through a hole.

Does she allow house pets?
No, she does not allow house pets.

His foul mouth puts him down again.
Did his foul mouth put him down again?

Karen got her gown from downtown.
Did Karen get her gown from downtown?

Some birds fly south in the winter.
Do some birds fly south in the winter?

The boxer bows out of the bout.
Did the boxer bow out of the bout?

The hotel will not allow loud noise.
No hotel will allow loud noise.

USE THE FOLLOWING WORDS IN SENTENCES:

towel	tower	owl	pout	allow
south	mouth	town	down	how

PART I

SECTION 9 – Additional Practice Words

And Reading Materials

LESSON 44

LESSON 44   ADDITIONAL PRACTICE ON TWO- AND THREE-SYLLABLE WORDS AND READING MATERIALS

READ THE FOLLOWING WORDS:

acquit	educate	ignore	obtain	ulcer
appear	escape	ivory	October	umpire
bakery	beckon	biceps	boxcar	buccaneer
balcony	behave	bingo	bottom	buffalo
canvas	census	cigar	compare	cultivate
daffodil	decade	diaper	dollar	duffel
dagger	deliver	dictator	domain	duster
family	fearful	figure	forbid	fury
favor	fever	finger	formula	future
gallon	gelatin	gigantic	gossip	gunfire
hammer	helmet	history	hospital	hurricane
janitor	jester	jitters	jogger	jubilee
katydid	kerosene	kidnap	Korea	Kuwait
ladder	legal	liquid	locate	luster
maintain	melody	midwife	mistake	muffin
naval	nectar	nipper	normal	nunnery
passenger	petticoat	pillar	popular	pursue
quarrel		quitter		
raisin	recite	riot	rotate	rusty
saliva	seldom	silver	solder	surname
taster	tempo	tinsel	tobacco	tunnel
vanish		victim	volume	
wagonload	weekend	widow	wombat	

USE THE FOLLOWING WORDS IN SENTENCES:

ladder	tobacco	riot	locate	surname
vanish	liquid	jester	passenger	pursue

We Can Do It

We sent men to the moon and back;
We have a spy eye in the sky that gazes at the stars;
We sent robots to test the alien soil of Mars for life;
With robot eyes we saw Jupiter and her moons up close;
We rescue objects in space and send them safely into orbit;
We dive into the ocean depths in tiny shells of metal and glass;
We span bays and great rivers;
We build towers so high that they scrape the belly of the sky;
We make smart bombs, so smart they can find small holes to squeeze into;
Why can't we make cars as others do?

A Haunted House?

The house is like any other house in the block. But for the green color and the wide windows, you can not tell it apart from other houses. If it is different, it is because eerie things take place inside.

The original owner sold the house after living there for less than a year. The second owner sold the house after living in it for three months. He said he had business in another city.

The new owners are a couple with two kids. After two months, there are murmurs among the neighbors. It is said that in the dead of night, you can hear voices in the living room. But no one is there. In the daytime, taps open and close. There seems to be someone in the kitchen. Lights go on and off. Backpacks, books, earrings, and other things disappear. They are found later in the most unlikely places.

One time when the two kids were alone at home, they saw a lady working in the kitchen. Wondering who she was, they went to the kitchen. She just disappeared. The two went to a neighbor and stayed there until their mom and dad came home from work. That was when all this talk started. Now, the question is: How long will the family last in the house?

More Than Money?

Peter goes to the park to enjoy a nice summer day. He rides his new bike and leaves it by a tree. He joins other boys at play. He forgets to keep an eye on his bike. When it is time to go home, his bike is gone.

Bess waits for the bus. As she waits, a man sits besides her inside the bus stop shed. Suddenly, the man grabs her purse and runs away with it. The purse did not contain much money but her credit cards were in it.

A man sips coffee at a table inside the SIT AND EAT. He looks at his watch. "Late again," he says to himself. He sits there waiting — five, ten, forty-five minutes. Finally, he gives up. He pays his bill and leaves.

Who lost the most? One can argue that Peter lost the most. To a boy, a new bike means a lot. Bess did not lose much. The man at SIT AND EAT did not lose anything either. Or did he?

Come to think of it, the man at SIT AND EAT may have lost more than the other two. Peter's bike and the money of Bess can be replaced. But the man's forty or more minutes is lost forever.

Some Tales Retold

The Turtle and the Eagle

High up on the mountain top, there lived an eagle. Down below, in the valley, lived a turtle.

The turtle often wondered: How does the valley look up on the mountain top? He knew, though, that he would never get to see the valley from the top.

One day the eagle came down and invited the turtle to go up to the top with him.

"But I can not fly like you or climb the mountain like a goat," the turtle said.

"Not to worry," replied the eagle. "See this stick? I will hold it with my claws and you bite it with your beak."

So up, up they flew. Near the top, the turtle looked down. How beautiful! he thought. He wanted to thank the eagle. The turtle opened his mouth, and down, down he went.

The Hare and the Turtle

The hare is fast and very proud of it. In fact, he brags about it often. Worse, he taunts the slower animals. Because the turtle is one of the slowest animals, he is often the target of the hare. "Make way slowpoke. You are so slow, you will kill anything you step on," the hare always says within the hearing of other animals. The hare's taunting is so bad that even other animals do not like it.

One day, the hare is in one of his mean moods and keeps taunting the turtle. "I can beat you in any race. One leg is all I need," he is saying. The monkey hears this and has an idea. Why not a race — a handicap race? The hare will use only one leg over a distance of one mile.

The hare quickly says, "Yes!" The turtle is prodded into it. But even with the handicap, the hare is heavily favored to win. The turtle is not given a ghost of a chance.

The day of the race comes. It seems that everything is in favor of the hare. The race course is over a hilly area. The starting line is at the foot of a hill. The road rises so high that it seems to meet the sky.

The gun barks. The hare is off quickly. Even on one leg, he hops to the top of the hill in no time. At the top he pauses. He looks back. He sees the turtle barely out of the starting line. He relaxes. He smiles. "It will take days before that slowpoke gets to the finish line," he says to himself. He hops. Suddenly, he stops. He rubs his eyes. He can not believe it. He sees a carrot patch. He detours. He eats and eats and eats until he gets a big, big bellyache.

His bellyache is so bad he is still doubled up at the carrot patch when the turtle crosses the finish line.

The Monkey and the Turtle

The monkey and the turtle were once very good friends. They worked together and played together. They took care of each other. What one had, he shared with the other.

One day they came upon a banana plant. It had fruit. As usual, they decided to share and divide it equally. They cut the plant in half. The monkey, wanting to put one over on the turtle, picked the half with the fruits. The turtle got the lower stem with the roots. The turtle did not say one word in protest.

After some time, the monkey visited his friend. He was in for a surprise! The turtle had banana plants all over his place. Some bore fruit, too!

The Wise Ass

There once was an ass who was very, very wise. His counsel was sought all over the animal kingdom. Even the owl, thought by many as a queer but wise bird, sought his counsel.

One time the king of the beasts came to him with a problem. The king looked haggard and tired from lack of sleep. He said, "I can hardly sleep at night. What must I do?"

The wise ass began to ask him questions. "Just what do you do in the daytime?"

"Oh," the lion said, "not much. I eat my fill, take long naps and laze around my jungle kingdom."

"Aha!" said the wise ass. "That is the cause of your problem. You overeat and you oversleep in the daytime. What you need is less food, some exercise, and no more naps in the daytime."

Following what the wise ass said, the king found that he could sleep soundly at night. The word got around and the ass became a famous ass. Soon gifts of food and other things were pouring in.

One day, he received two bundles of hay. One was placed to his left, the other to his right.

Both looked appetizing. He debated with himself: "Which one will I eat first?" For every reason he had for eating the one on the left first, he also had a reason for eating the one on the right first. He debated and debated until he died.

Part I

SECTION 10 – Suffixes and Exercises

LESSON 45

LESSON 45

SUFFIXES

Adding suffixes — Suffixes are word endings which change the function or meaning of words to which they are added.

EXAMPLE: ING, ER, ED, ES, EST, EN
                  like / make / joke / hike

1) When adding ING to a base word ending in E, drop the vowel E and add the suffix ING.

EXAMPLE: like = lik + ing = liking   make = mak + ing = making
               joke = jok + ing = joking   line = lin + ing = lining

The same is true when suffixes that begin with E, like ED, ER, ES are added.

EXAMPLE: like = lik + ed = liked   make = mak + er = maker
               joke = jok + ed = jokes   line = lin + es = lines

EXERCISES:

BASE WORD + ING	ER	ED	ES	EST	EN
hike = hik + hiking	hiker	hiked	hikes	X_____	X_____
give	_____	X_____	_____	X_____	_____
tame	_____	_____	_____	_____	X_____
wade	_____	_____	_____	X_____	X_____
move	_____	_____	_____	X_____	X_____
pose	_____	_____	_____	X_____	X_____
reduce	_____	_____	_____	X_____	X_____
bake	_____	_____	_____	X_____	X_____
leave	_____	X_____	X_____	_____	X_____	X_____
weave	_____	_____	_____	_____	X_____	X_____

(See answers on page 66.)

2) When the last three letters have the consonant-vowel-consonant pattern, as in the words below:

cut, gag, hit, debug,

the final consonant is doubled before adding the suffixes.

cut = cutt + ing = cutting   gag = gagg + ed = gagged
hit = hitt + er = hitter   debug = debugg + ed = debugged

EXERCISES:

BASE WORD + ING	ER	ED	ES/S	EST	EN
pat = patt + patting	X_____	patted	X_____	X_____	X_____
rap	_____	_____	X_____	X_____	X_____
pet	_____	X_____	_____	X_____	X_____	X_____
pen	_____	X_____	_____	X_____	X_____	X_____
hit	_____	_____	X_____	X_____	X_____	X_____
sit	_____	_____	X_____	X_____	X_____	X_____
dot	_____	X_____	_____	X_____	X_____	X_____
bog	_____	X_____	_____	X_____	X_____	X_____
bug	_____	X_____	_____	X_____	X_____	X_____
gut	_____	_____	_____	X_____	X_____	X_____

(See answers on page 66.)

EXCEPTION:　　　When the last three letters have the consonant-vowel-consonant pattern, but the last letter is a Y, do not double the Y.
Add ING, ER, ED, and S to the root word.
EXAMPLE:

play = play + ing = playing　　　　play = play + er = player
play = play + ed = played　　　　　play = play + s = plays

EXERCISES:

BASE WORD + ING	ER	ED	ES/S	EST	EN
coy = coy +　X____	coyer	X____	X____	coyest	X____
buy　____	____	X____	____	X____	X____
decoy　____	X____	____	____	X____	X____
convey　____	____	____	____	X____	X____
delay　____	X____	____	____	X____	X____
obey　____	X____	____	____	X____	X____

(See answers on page 66.)

3) When the base word ends in a consonant but does not fall into the consonant-vowel-consonant pattern, add the suffixes without changing the spelling of the base word.

EXAMPLE:　　　feed / add / eat / fish
After adding the suffixes:
feed = feed + er = feeder　　　　add = add + ing = adding
fish = fish + es = fishes　　　　　eat = eat + en = eaten

EXERCISES:

BASE WORD + ING	ER	ED	ES	EST	EN
mash = mash + mashing	masher	mashed	mashes	X____	X____
beat　____	____	X____	X____	X____	____
feel　____	____	X____	X____	X____	X____
deal　____	____	X____	X____	X____	X____
seal　____	____	____	X____	X____	X____
call　____	____	____	X____	X____	X____
butt　____	____	____	X____	X____	X____
end　____	X____	____	X____	X____	X____
hard　X____	____	X____	X____	____	____

(See answers on page 66.)

4) When the last letter is a Y and it is preceded by a consonant, the Y in the base word is changed into I before adding the suffixes beginning with E:

EXAMPLE:　　　dry / jelly / cry / soggy
Drop the Y and add I:
　　　　dry = dr + i　　jelly = jell + i　　cry = cr + i　　　soggy = sogg + i
Then add suffixes ED, ES, ER, EST, EN:
　　　　dri + ed = dried　jelli + es = jellies
　　　　cri + er = cried　　　　　　　　　soggi + est = soggiest
The suffix ING is simply added to the root word in appropriate cases as in:
　　　　dry + ing = drying　cry + ing = crying

EXERCISES:

BASE WORDS	+ ING	ER	ED	ES	EST	EN
deny = deni	denying	denier	denied	denies	X_____	X_____
silly	X_____	_____	X_____	X_____	_____	X_____
rely	_____	X_____	_____	_____	X_____	X_____
rally	_____	X_____	_____	_____	X_____	X_____
tally	_____	_____	_____	_____	X_____	X_____
empty (*v*)	_____	X_____	_____	_____	X_____	X_____
empty (*adj*)	X_____	_____	X_____	X_____	_____	X_____
tarry	_____	_____	_____	_____	X_____	X_____
tardy	X_____	_____	X_____	X_____	_____	X_____
comely	X_____	_____	X_____	X_____	_____	X_____

(See answers on page 66.)

Suffixes — Answers to Exercises

1.

give	giving	giver		gives	given
tame	taming	tamer	tamed	tames	
wade	wading	wader	waded	wades	
move	moving	mover	moved	moves	
pose	posing	poser	posed	poses	
reduce	reducing	reducer	reduced	reduces	
bake	baking	baker	baked	bakes	
leave	leaving			leaves	
weave	weaving	weaver	weaved	weaves	

2.

rap	rapping	rapper	rapped
pet	petting		petted
pen	penning		penned
hit	hitting	hitter	
sit	sitting	sitter	
dot	dotting		dotted
bog	bogging		bogged
bug	bugging		bugged
gut	gutting	gutter	gutted

3.

buy	buying	buyer		buys
decoy			decoyed	decoys
convey	conveying	conveyer	conveyed	conveys
delay	delaying		delayed	delays
obey	obeying		obeyed	obeys

4.

beat	beating	beater			beaten
feel	feeling	feeler			
deal	dealing	dealer			
seal	sealing	sealer	sealed		
call	calling	caller	called		
butt	butting	butter	butted		
end	ending		ended		
hard		harder		hardest	harden

5.

silly		sillier		silliest	
rely	relying		relied	relies	
rally	rallying		rallied	rallies	
tally	tallying	tallier	tallied	tallies	
empty (v)	emptying		emptied	empties	
empty (a)		emptier		emptiest	
tarry	tarrying	tarrier	tarried	tarries	
tardy		tardier		tardiest	
comely		comelier		comeliest	

PART II

SECTION 1 – L Blends

LESSONS 46-49

LESSON 46   BL as in blaze

READ AND WRITE THE FOLLOWING WORDS

black	bleak	blind	blow	bluff
blade	bleed	blizzard	block	blush
blame	blemish	blink	blond	blunt
blank	blend	blister	blot	blood

house	oyster	auto	book	moose

blouse				blue
				blew
				bloom

READ THE FOLLOWING SENTENCES:

His bluff did not work.
Did his bluff work?

Can the bleach remove the blemish?
Yes, the bleach can remove the blemish.

The smoke from the blaze made Dennis blink.
Did the smoke from the blaze make Dennis blink?

Dennis will buy a block of ice.
Will Dennis buy a block of ice?
Dennis lives down the block.

Sam's blind date is a blonde.
Is Sam's blind date a blonde?

A blizzard causes a blackout in the city.
Did a blizzard cause a blackout in the city?

The blank tapes are atop the black desk.
Are the blank tapes atop the black desk?

USE THE FOLLOWING WORDS IN SENTENCES:

blade	blame	blush	blister	bloom

CL as in clover

READ AND WRITE THE FOLLOWING WORDS:

clay	clean	climb	clock	club
clap	clear	click	close	clung
clamp	clerk	clip	clot	clutter
clash	clever	cling	clog	clump

house	oyster	auto	book	moose

clown	cloy	claw		clue
cloud				

READ THE FOLLOWING SENTENCES:

Don will clean the club house.
Will Don clean the club house?

On a clear day you can see the tower.
Can you see the tower on a clear day?

Do you have to be clever to be a clown?
Yes, you have to be clever to be a clown.

The clerk clutters his desk with paper and clips.
Does the clerk clutter his desk with paper and clips?
Do not clip his hair too close to the skin.

The clock fell from the table.
Did the clock fall from the table?

Does the town house open at 8 o'clock?
Yes, the town house opens at 8 o'clock.

Close the door behind you.
How close are we to the town?
We are not even close to the town.

USE THE FOLLOWING WORDS IN SENTENCES:

cloud	claw	clay	clog	clue

LESSON 47   FL as in flower

READ AND WRITE THE FOLLOWING WORDS:

flame	flea	flicker	float	fluffy
flag	fleece	flies	flow	flush
flat	fleet	flip	flock	flutter
flash	flesh	fling	flop	flood

house	oyster	auto	book	moose

flour	flaw		flew
flounder	floor		fluid
			flute

READ THE FOLLOWING SENTENCES:

The bee flies from flower to flower.
Does the bee fly from flower to flower?

A bag of flour is on the floor.
Is that a bag of flour on the floor?

The flame flickers and dies.
Did the flame flicker and die?

Flash floods cause delays.
Did flash floods cause delays?

A fleet of boats go out to sea.
Did a fleet of boats go out to sea?

Can you flag down a taxi for me?
Yes, I will flag down a taxi for you.

A flock of swans are by the lake.
Is a flock of swans by the lake?
Swans flock in the lake to feed.

The boat floats with the flow of the river.
Does the boat float with the flow of the river?

USE THE FOLLOWING WORDS IN SENTENCES:

flounder	flaw	fluid	floor	flood

GL as in glider

READ AND WRITE THE FOLLOWING WORDS:

glad	gleam	glitter	glow	glum
glamor	glean	glide	global	glutton
glass	glen	glimpse	globe	glove
glance	glee	glimmer	glory	

house	oyster	auto	book	moose

				glue
				gloom

READ THE FOLLOWING SENTENCES:

The glee club is glad to sing here.
Is the glee club glad it will sing here?

Did the glider glide down the field?
The glider glides down the field.

Is there a glimmer of hope for the sick?
Yes, there is a glimmer of hope for the sick.

Glue will work on glass.
Will glue work on glass?

The last global war was a glimpse of hell.
Was the last global war a glimpse of hell?

Global warming worries savants.
Does global warming worry savants?

The glitter and glamor of Hollywood does not appeal to her.
Does not the glitter and glamor of Hollywood appeal to her?

USE THE FOLLOWING WORDS IN SENTENCES:

glue	glass	glide	gloom	globe

LESSON 48   PL as in plate

READ AND WRITE THE FOLLOWING WORDS:

place	please	pliers	explode	plug
plain	plenty	supply	plover	plum
plant	pleasure	reply	plod	plumber
plastic		apply	plot	plunder

house	oyster	auto	book	moose

plow

READ THE FOLLOWING SENTENCES:

There is a picnic place up on the hill.
Is there a picnic place up in the hill?

We need plenty of paper plates for the party.
Do we need plenty of paper plates for the party?

Plow the land before you plant it.
Before you plant the land, plow it.

The plot to depose the king fails.
Did the plot to depose the king fail?
Peas are planted in the plot.

They call her plain Jane to tease her.
Do they call her plain Jane to tease her?

Does the plumber need the pliers?
The plumber needs the pliers.

Please get a plastic bag for the plums.
Yes, here is a plastic bag for the plums.

USE THE FOLLOWING WORDS IN SENTENCES:

plastic	plow	apply	plug	pleasure

SL as in slippers

READ AND WRITE THE FOLLOWING WORDS:

slay	sled	slide	slow	slushy
slave	slender	slippery	slope	slug
slack	sleep	sling	slog	slugger
sleigh	sleeve	slip	sloppy	slumber

house	oyster	auto	book	moose

slouch	slaughter		sloop
			slew

READ THE FOLLOWING SENTENCES:

The lineman slings the slack line to the pole.
Did the lineman sling the slack line to the pole?

His slippers are by the slide.
Are his slippers by the slide?
The runner slides safely home.

The garden slug is very slow animal.
Is the garden slug a very slow animal?

Slow down, the road is very slippery.
It is slippery down the road, go slow.

Icy rain made the roads slippery.
Did icy rain make the roads slippery?

The slave is in deep sleep.
Is the slave in deep sleep?

Can I take a sleigh ride to town?
Yes, you can take a sleigh ride to town.

USE THE FOLLOWING WORDS IN SENTENCES:

slay	slouch	sloop	slugger	sloppy

LESSON 49   SPL as in splash

READ AND WRITE THE FOLLOWING WORDS:

splatter	spleen	splice	splotch	splutter
	splendid	splint		
	splendor	splinter		

READ THE FOLLOWING SENTENCES:

Can the old man splice the ropes?
Yes, the old man can splice the ropes?

Soap and water will remove all the splotches.
Will soap and water remove all the splotches?

Banana splits sell well in summer.
Do banana splits sell well in summer?
The winners will split the money two ways.

Don splashed and splattered oil on the canvas.
Did Don splash and splatter oil on the canvas?

Bruce used a piece of wood as a splint.
Did Bruce use a piece of wood as a splint?

The tiger has a splinter in its paw.
Does the tiger have a splinter in its paw?

USE THE FOLLOWING WORDS IN SENTENCES:

splash	splatter	splendid	splice	splutter

PART II

SECTION 2 – R Blends

LESSONS 50-53

LESSON 50   BR as in brush

READ AND WRITE THE FOLLOWING WORDS:

brain	breed	bridle	bronco	brunch
brake	breeze	brick	bronze	brother
brave	bread	bring	broccoli	
break	breath	brine	broke	

house	oyster	auto	book	moose

brown	broil	brawn		broom
		brawl		bruise
				Bruce

READ THE FOLLOWING SENTENCES:

Bruce put the bridle on the bronco.
Did Bruce put the bridle on the bronco?

The car brakes and the wiper blades are new.
Are the car brakes and the wiper blades new?

Bruce will bring a new brush.
Will Bruce bring a new brush?

Bruce had bread and soup for brunch.
Did Bruce have bread and soup for brunch?

A breeze blows away the mist.
Did a breeze blow away the mist?

There is no damage to the brick house.
Is there damage to the brick house?

Bronze was made into weapons
   and tools during the Bronze Age.
Was bronze made into tools
   and weapons during the Bronze Age?

Bruce and Joe are brothers.
Joe, his brother, will ride the bronco.

USE THE FOLLOWING WORDS IN SENTENCES:

brown	brawl	broom	breeze	bruise

CR as in crab

READ AND WRITE THE FOLLOWING WORDS:

crack	cream	crib	crow	crumb
crane	creel	crier	croak	crush
cramp	creek	crick	crop	crutch
crayfish	credit	crime	crocus	crust

house	oyster	auto	book	moose

crown		crawl	crook	crew
crouch		crawfish		crude
crowd				cruise
				cruel

READ THE FOLLOWING SENTENCES:

Can you crack the oyster shell?
The crack in the wall is bigger now.
Is the crack in the wall bigger now?

It is time to harvest the crops in the field.
Is it time to harvest the crops in the field?

At this time of the year,
   the creek is full of crayfish.
Is the creek full of crayfish
   at this time of the year?

A crick is a cramp at the back of the neck.
Is a crick a cramp at the back of the neck?

The fisherman has some crabs in his creel.
Does the fisherman have some crabs in his creel?

The crow pecks at the bread crumbs.
Is the crow pecking at the bread crumbs?

A crowd has come to see the crown.
Has a crowd come to see the crown?

USE THE FOLLOWING WORDS IN SENTENCES:

crude   cruel   credit   crutch   crime

LESSON 51 DR as in dragon

READ AND WRITE THE FOLLOWING WORDS:

drain	dread	drive	drone	drub
draft	dream	drip	drop	drum
drape	dreary	drift	drove	drunk
draught	drench	drink	drover	drug

house	oyster	auto	book	moose

drown		draw	drew
drowsy		drawl	droop
		drawn	drool

READ THE FOLLOWING SENTENCES:

The drover drives his herd of cows to market.
Did the drover drive his herd of cows to market?

Will drugs ruin your life?
Yes, drugs will ruin your life.

The policy is to curb drunk driving.
Is the policy to curb drunk driving?

The game ended in a draw.
Did the game end in a draw?
Can you draw a dragon?

He dreams of snakes and dragons.
Do you always dream of snakes and dragons?

Be careful not to drop the drum.
There is a drop of cream on the drum.

"If you drink, do not drive,"
  makes a lot of sense.
Does, "If you drink, do not drive,"
  make a lot of sense?

The drive to raise money
  for the poor is a success.

There is a draft coming from the window.
Is the draft coming from the window?

USE THE FOLLOWING WORDS IN SENTENCES:

drown	drench	drawl	dread	drift

FR as in freezer

READ AND WRITE THE FOLLOWING WORDS:

frail	freedom	fried	frog
frank	freak	frisk	frozen
frame	fresh	fright	front
freight	French	fringe	frost

house	oyster	auto	book	moose

frown	fraud	fruit

READ THE FOLLOWING SENTENCES:

Fresh fruits and fried fish were
  served for lunch.
Were fresh fruits and fried fish
  served for lunch?

We need frank men and fresh ideas.
Do we need frank men and fresh ideas?

Tadpoles become frogs.
Do tadpoles become frogs?

All men desire freedom if they can have it.
Do all men desire freedom if they can have it?

Ice cream is a frozen delight.
Is ice cream a frozen delight?

Did you leave the key at the front desk?
The front desk is not taken yet.

The freight car has a freezer for frozen items.
Does the freight car have a freezer
  for frozen items?

The fruits were ruined by frost.
Did frost ruin the fruits?

USE THE FOLLOWING WORDS IN SENTENCES:

frame	freak	frog	fresh	front

LESSON 52 GR as in grape

READ AND WRITE THE FOLLOWING WORDS:

great	grief	grit	grow	grub
gravel	grease	grin	grocer	grudge
graze	greet	grill	groggy	gruff
grass	green	gripe	grope	grumpy

growl	group
ground	grew
grouse	

READ THE FOLLOWING SENTENCES:

A herd of goats grazes near the water hole.
Is a herd of goats grazing near the water hole?

The valley grows grapes for wine making.
Does the valley grow grapes for wine making?

Labor gripes about low wages.
Does labor gripe about low wages?

The grocer greets everyone with a wide grin.
Does the grocer greet everyone with a wide
  grin?

Do we have gravel for the roadway?
Yes, we have gravel for the roadway.

The car needs grease and oil.
Does the car need grease and oil?

Goats love to eat green grass.
Do goats love to eat green grass?

A grudge is a heavy load to carry around.
Is a grudge a heavy load to carry around?

USE THE FOLLOWING WORDS IN SENTENCES:

growl　　　　　　　group　　　　　　ground　　　　　great　　　　　grumpy

PR as in pretzel

READ AND WRITE THE FOLLOWING WORDS:

pray	preach	price	prom
praise	present	prick	problem
prank	predict	pride	profit
prance	pressure	prince	product

proud	prawn	prove
prowler		proof
prowess		prudent

READ THE FOLLOWING SENTENCES:

"Pray and praise the Lord," said the preacher.

Did the preacher say,
    "Pray and praise the Lord"?

A lower price on this product
    means more profit.
Will a lower price on this product
    mean more profit?

Is there proof that he is the prowler?
No, there is no proof that he is the prowler.

The prince was not present at the ball.

At the ball, the prince gave her a present.

The prince will present her at the ball.

The problem will pressure the mayor to act.

Will the problem pressure the mayor to act?

The tire pressure is too low.
Is the tire pressure too low?

USE THE FOLLOWING WORDS IN SENTENCES:

praise	prank	probe	prom	prove

LESSON 53   TR as in tree

READ AND WRITE THE FOLLOWING WORDS:

trace	treat	trial	trot	truck
train	trench	trinket	trombone	trumpet
trade	tread	triple	trophy	trunk
travel	treasure	trigger	tropics	

trout		trawl		troop
trowel		trawler		truce
				true
				truly

READ THE FOLLOWING SENTENCES:

The team trains before it travels.

The coach and the team travel by train.

Do the coach and the team travel by train?

Will Don trade his trombone for a trumpet?

Yes, Don will trade his trombone for a trumpet.

Don can not cope with the heat of the tropics.

Can Don cope with the heat of the tropics?

The trunk is full of trinkets.

Is the trunk full of trinkets?

The troops entered into a truce.

Did the troops enter into a truce?

Is travel truly an eye opener?

Yes, travel is truly an eye opener?

The truck fell into a trench.

Did the truck fall into a trench?

There is a lot of treasure under the sea.

Treasure the sea and treat it well.

USE THE FOLLOWING WORDS IN SENTENCES:

trout	true	trigger	trace	trial

SCR as in scraper

READ AND WRITE THE FOLLOWING WORDS:

scrape	scream	scribe	scrod	scrub
scraggy	screen	scribble	scroll	
scramble	screech	scrip		
scratch		script		

scrawl	screw

READ THE FOLLOWING SENTENCES:

Tom screams in fear.
Did Tom scream in fear?

Did Ben scrub the floor?
Yes, Ben scrubbed the floor.

Bruce scraped his neck on a wire.
Did Bruce scrape his neck on a wire?

The cat scratches the screen.
Does the cat scratch the screen?

The script calls for a grumpy old man.
Does the script call for a grumpy old man?

The scribe scribbles a note on a piece of paper.
Did the scribe scribble a note on a piece of paper?

The Navy will scrap some of the old boats.
Will the Navy scrap some of the old boats?

Can you screw back the screen?
Yes, I can screw back the screen.

Will you broil the scrod?
Yes, I will broil the scrod.

USE THE FOLLOWING WORDS IN SENTENCES:

scraper	scroll	screen	scrape	scrawl

PART II

SECTION 3 – S Blends

LESSONS 54-59

LESSON 54   SC = SK as in scale

READ AND WRITE THE FOLLOWING WORDS:

scan	scold	scull
scatter	scope	scuffle
scalp	score	sculpt
scamper	scorpion	sculptor
scare		
scarce		

scout	scoop
scowl	scoot

READ THE FOLLOWING SENTENCES:

In the scuffle, scores of fans were injured.
Were scores of fans injured in the scuffle?
Bruce scored the only goal for his team.

The sculptor scans his work.
Is the sculptor scanning his work?

The scouts are near the foot of the hill.
He scouts the foot of the hill to
    see to it that all is clear.

The leaves scatter in the wind.
Did the leaves scatter in the wind?

The unruly boys were scolded.
Were the unruly boys scolded?

Can you give me a scoop of rice?
Yes, here is a scoop of rice.

The team scored a win in the scull race.
Did the team score a win in the scull race?

The scorpion scoots and hides under the rock.
Did the scorpion scoot and hide under the rock?

USE THE FOLLOWING WORDS IN SENTENCES:

scalp	sculpt	scamper	scarf	scare

LESSON 55   SCH = SK as in school, SK as in skeleton

READ AND WRITE THE FOLLOWING WORDS:

skate	schedule	skid	scholar	skunk
skein	scheme	skill		skull
	sketch	skillet		skew
		skim		skewer
		skin		
		skipper		

schooner

READ THE FOLLOWING SENTENCES:

Do you have the schedule of the
  schooner for today?

The schooner is scheduled to arrive today.

Is the schooner scheduled to arrive today?

The school system supports scholars.

Does the school system support scholars?

Other animals do not eat the skunk
  because of its bad smell.

The bad smell of the skunk makes it
  less likely to be eaten by other animals.

The skate is a fish with a wide body.

Bruce skates to exercise.

Do not skate in the street.

Skeletons, skulls, and scrolls were
  found in the cave.

Were skeletons, skulls, and scrolls
  found in the cave?

The success of the scheme depends on timing.

Does the success of the scheme
  depend on timing?

The skewers are by the grill.

Are the skewers by the grill?

The skill of the skippers will decide
  the boat races.

Will the skill of the skippers decide
  the boat races?

USE THE FOLLOWING WORDS IN SENTENCES:

skate	skunk	sketch	skipper	skein

LESSON 56   SM as in smoke

READ AND WRITE THE FOLLOWING WORDS:

smack	smear	smile	smoking	smudge
smash	smelt	smirk	smock	smug
	smell	smith	smog	smuggle
		smite	smolder	

	small	smooth

READ THE FOLLOWING SENTENCES:

There are small ducks in the lake.
Are there small ducks in the lake?

The fire is smoldering under all that smoke.
Is the fire smoldering under all that smoke?

The smelting plant emits so much smoke.
Does the smelting plant emit so much smoke?
The smelt is a small fish.

The blacksmith's overalls are
   smeared with soot.
Are the blacksmith's overalls
smeared with soot?

Smoking will ruin your health.
Will smoking ruin your health?

The smoke is coming from the house.
Do not smoke inside the house.

A smile can get you some place, a frown cannot.
She smiles and my day is made.
After the win, the team is all smiles.

His smock is full of greasy smudges.
Is his smock full of greasy smudges?

Use your brain, don't use drugs.
Drugs kill, don't use drugs.

USE THE FOLLOWING WORDS IN SENTENCES:

smooth	smuggle	smock	smear	smack

LESSON 57   SN as in snail

READ AND WRITE THE FOLLOWING WORDS:

snack	sneak	snicker	snob	snub
snag	sneaker	sniffle	snore	snuff
snake	sneeze	snipe	snorkel	snuggle
snap	sneer	snip	snow	

snout   snoop

READ THE FOLLOWING SENTENCES:

The wind snuffs out the flame.
Does the wind snuff out the flame?

Pollen makes him sniffle and sneeze.
Does pollen make him sniffle and sneeze?

Did the snake crawl into a hole in the ground?
Yes, the snake crawled into a hole in the
    ground.
Snipes also feed on snails and small snakes.
Do snipes also feed on snails and small snakes?

A gunman snipes from the tower.
Is the gunman sniping from the tower?

He snuggles close to the fireplace.
Did he snuggle close to the fire place?

Tom will buy new sneakers.
Is Tom buying new sneakers?

Tom's snack is on top of the table.
Is Tom's snack on top of the table?

The fisherman's hook snags on a rock.
Is the fisherman's hook snagged on a rock?

USE THE FOLLOWING WORDS IN SENTENCES:

snack   snip   snow   snorkel   snout

SP as in spoon

READ AND WRITE THE FOLLOWING WORDS:

space	special	spice	spoke	sputter
spade	speech	spider	sponge	spud
spank	speak	spine	spot	spun
spat	spell	spin		Sputnik

spout	spawn	spook
spouse		spool

READ THE FOLLOWING SENTENCES:

The Sputnik was the first man-made
   object in space.
Was the Sputnik the first man-made
   object in space?

Bess needs a special brace for her spine.
Does Bess need a special brace for her spine?

The quest for spices led to great discoveries.
Did the quest for spices lead to
   great discoveries?

Can you spell "spouse"?
Her spouse can not spell "spawn."

The speech has only one useful idea.
Does the speech have only one useful idea?

Sponge comes from the sea.
Does sponge come from the sea?
The nurse gives the sick man a sponge bath.

The web the spider spins is a home and a trap.
Is the web the spider spins a home and a trap?

USE THE FOLLOWING WORDS IN SENTENCES:

speak	spook	spool	spawn	sputter

LESSON 58   SPR as in spring

READ AND WRITE THE FOLLOWING WORDS:

sprain	spread	sprites	sprocket	sprung
sprang	spree	sprinkle		
spray		sprint		
		sprinter		

sprout   sprawl   spruce

READ THE FOLLOWING SENTENCES:

The sprinter sprains his ankle.

Did the sprinter sprain his ankle?

With a sprain, the sprinter can not run the race.

Bruce sprinkles the sprouts with water.

Did Bruce sprinkle the sprouts with water?

Sprites exist only in fairy tales.

Do sprites exist only in fairy tales?

The spruce grows new sprouts.

Does the spruce grow new sprouts?

Bruce spruces up for the party.

Winter lingers, but spring is close behind.

The tiger springs at its prey.

The spring on the clock is broken.

The sprat is a small herring.

A small herring is called a sprat.

The sprawling spread lies east of the river.

Does the sprawling spread lie east of river?

USE THE FOLLOWING WORDS IN SENTENCES:

spray   spread   sprocket   spree   sprint

SQU = SKW as in squirrel

READ AND WRITE THE FOLLOWING WORDS:

squat	squeak	squid
squad	squeal	squirm
squander	squeeze	squint
square	squelch	squirt
squash		

squaw
squawk
squall

READ THE FOLLOWING SENTENCES:

He squanders his money on foolish buys.
Does he squander his money on foolish buys?

The squash looks like a pumpkin.
Does the squash look like a pumpkin?
Don't sit on the pumpkin or you will squash it.

A squall sinks the boat.
Did a squall sink the boat?

Squatters take over the square.
Did the squatters take over the square?

The squid squirts black ink and escapes.
Did the squid squirt black ink and escape?

Take a squad of men and retake
  the square from the squatters.
Am I to retake the square from the squatters
  with a squad of men?

Can you squeeze out the juice from this fruit?
Sure, I will squeeze out the juice from the fruit.

USE THE FOLLOWING WORDS IN SENTENCES:

squirrel   squeal   squeak   squaw   squall

LESSON 59   ST as in steamship

READ AND WRITE THE FOLLOWING WORDS:

steak	steam	stick	stove	stew
stable	stem	sting	stock	stub
stack	steep	still	stone	stuff
stand	steer	style	stomach	stun

stout	stall		student
			stoop
			studio

READ THE FOLLOWING SENTENCES:

The steamship steams out to the sea.
Did the steamship steam out to the sea?

The stack of boxes is not stable.
Is the stack of boxes not stable?
Is the stable clean?

Make a stand, say no to drugs.
Saying no to drugs is a good stand.
There is no paper in the stand.

The beef stew is still in the stove.
Is the beef stew still in the stove?

The students pay a steep price for books.
Do the students pay a steep price for books?

Sit still or the bee will sting you.
The bee sting still hurts.
Does the bee sting still hurt?

Bruce stubs his big toe on a stone.
Did Bruce stub his big toe on a stone?
Did you keep the ticket stub?

USE THE FOLLOWING WORDS IN SENTENCES:

stout	stall	student	studio	stood

STR as in string

READ AND WRITE THE FOLLOWING WORDS:

strap	streak	strive	strove	strut
strand	stream	strip	stroke	struggle
strain	street	strike	strong	strum
strange	stress	strict	stroller	

straw

READ AND WRITE THE FOLLOWING SENTENCES:

The street by the river is full of strollers.

Is the street by the river full of strollers?

Bill is strong in backstroke.

Is Bill strong in backstroke?

Is the struggle for freedom easy?

The struggle for freedom is never easy.

A frail man struggles for freedom.

Is it not strange that the street
  is empty at this time?

Indeed, it is strange that the street
  is empty at this time.

Do not clog the stream with straw.

The straw will clog the stream.

Do all animals have mean streaks?

All animals have mean streaks.

Labor feels the stress and strain of the strike.

The batter strikes out again.

A strict law is needed to keep the stream clean.

To keep the stream clean, a strict law is
  needed.

USE THE FOLLOWING WORDS IN SENTENCES:

strap	stride	stroke	strut	strum

PART II

SECTION 4 – W Blends

LESSON 60

LESSON 60
TW as in twin

READ AND WRITE THE FOLLOWING WORDS:

twang   tweed   twice
               tweezers   twiddle
               twelve   twig
               twenty   twilight
                              twinkle
                              twist
                              twitter

READ THE FOLLOWING SENTENCES:

Robert twiddles the twig.
Does Robert twiddle the twig?

Robert has two tweed jackets.
Does Robert have two tweed jackets?

Twelve citizens sit in a jury.
Do twelve citizens sit in a jury?
Twelve makes a dozen, doesn't it?

How can you tell one twin from the other?
You can tell one twin from the other
  by a mole on the face.

Bruce speaks with a twang.
Does Bruce speak with a twang?

Twice ten equals twenty, true?
Yes, ten taken twice is twenty.

The wire will break if you twist it.
Don't twist the wire or it will break.
Can you dance the Twist?

The city has twin towers.
Use the tweezers to pull the splinter out.
Can you pull the splinter out with a tweezers?

USE THE FOLLOWING WORDS IN SENTENCES:

twenty   twig   twinkle   tweed   twitter

DW as in dwarf
GU = GW, GW as in Gwen

READ AND WRITE THE FOLLOWING WORDS:

dwarf	dwell	dwindle
dwarves	dwelling	Dwight
guano		Guinevere
guava		
Guam		
Guadalcanal		
Guatemala		

READ THE FOLLOWING SENTENCES:

In one's heart, a monster or an angel can dwell.
Can a monster or angel dwell in one's heart?

A dwarf of a man, he is mean and cruel.
He is mean and cruel, a dwarf of a man.

Hope dwindles for quake survivors.
Has hope dwindled for quake survivors?

Guinevere was King Arthur's wife.
Was Guinevere King Arthur's wife?

Dwight's dwelling is by the sea
Is the dwelling by the sea owned by Dwight.

Guano is the manure of sea birds.
The manure of sea birds is called guano.

Guam and Guadalcanal are in the Pacific.
Are Guam and Guadalcanal in the Pacific?

Gwen likes guavas.
Does Gwen like guavas?

A seven footer, Arthur dwarfs Gwen.
Gwen looks like a dwarf besides Arthur,
    a seven footer.

USE THE FOLLOWING WORDS IN SENTENCES:

dwarf	guano	guavas	dwindle	dwell

PART II

SECTION 5 – Digraphs

LESSONS 61-65

LESSON 61

CH as in chair

READ AND WRITE THE FOLLOWING WORDS:

chain	cheap	chicken	choke	chubby
chase	cheek	chick	chose	church
change	chess	child	chocolate	chug
chat	chief	chimney	chop	chunk

chow	choice	
chowder		chew
		choose

READ THE FOLLOWING SENTENCES:

In chess the goal is to mate the king.
Is the goal in chess to mate the king?

The child chokes on the chocolate.
Did the child choke on the chocolate?

Bess likes chicken soup better than oysters.
Does Bess like chicken soup better than oysters?

As a child, he went to church every Sunday.
Every Sunday the child goes to church.

Peter likes clam chowder.
Does Peter like clam chowder?

Will you change your choice?
No, I will not change my choice.

Bruce chops wood for the stove.
Did Bruce chop wood for the stove?

The key chain is on top of the chair.
Is the key chain on top of the chair?

USE THE FOLLOWING WORDS IN SENTENCES:

chew	choose	chair	cheap	change

CH = K as in mechanic

READ AND WRITE THE FOLLOWING WORDS:

chameleon	chemist	Christmas	chorus
chaos	ocher	christen	cholera
Bach		choir	chlorine
character			loch
ache			echo

READ THE FOLLOWING SENTENCES:

Did Bach make music for the chorus?
Yes, Bach made music for the chorus.

The mechanic will fix the auto.
Will the mechanic fix the auto?

It was chaos in the city during the riots.
Did the riots cause chaos in the city?

Cholera is a dreadful disease.
Is cholera a dreadful disease?

Will chlorine purify water?
Yes, chlorine will purify water.

The choir will sing on Christmas day.
Will the choir sing on Christmas day?

The chameleon can change its color.
Can the chameleon change its color?

USE THE FOLLOWING WORDS IN SENTENCES:

character   ache   echo   loch   mechanic

LESSON 62

PH = F as in telephone

READ AND WRITE THE FOLLOWING WORDS:

pharaoh	Phoenix	philosopher	phobia
phantom	pheasant		phony
pharmacy	phlegm		phonics
	phoebe		phonograph
			photo
			phlox

READ THE FOLLOWING SENTENCES:

The photo album is for the baby.
Is the photo album for the baby?

Is phonics one way to learn how to read?
Yes, phonics is one way to learn how to read.

Is the pharmacy open until five today?
No, the pharmacy is closed for the day.

Is the phoebe a big bird?
No, the phoebe is a very small bird.

The phony bill looks real.
Does the phony bill look real?

Does phlegm clog his throat?
Phlegm clogs his throat.

It is said that a philosopher is a blind man
  looking for a black cat in a dark cellar, and
  his problem is that the black cat is not in the
  cellar. Is this true?

Is phlox a flower?
Yes, phlox is a flower.

USE THE FOLLOWING WORDS IN SENTENCES:

phobia	telephone	phantom	pheasant	phoebe

LESSON 63
SH as in shell

READ AND WRITE THE FOLLOWING WORDS:

shabby	shed	shift	show	shuttle
shake	shelter	shiver	shock	shudder
shape	sheep	shine	shop	shut
sharp	shear	ship	shore	shun

shout		shawl		shoe
shower		Shawn		shoot
				shook

READ THE FOLLOWING SENTENCES:

The animal shelter puts some dogs to sleep.
Does the animal shelter put some dogs to sleep?

There is a shuttle bus that goes to town.
Is there a shuttle bus that goes to town?

Snakes and lizards shed their skins.
Do snakes and lizards shed their skins?
There is a snake skin inside the tool shed.

Shawn shears the sheep's wool.
Did Shawn shear the sheep's wool?

Shawn is not in shape for his bout.
Is Shawn in shape for his bout?

The ship is headed for the reefs.
Is the ship headed for the reefs?

Shawn is taking a shower.
Is Shawn taking a shower?
They gave the bride-to-be a shower.

The seashore is full of seashells.
Is the seashore full of seashells?

USE THE FOLLOWING WORDS IN SENTENCES:

shake	shout	shoe	shoot	shock

CH = SH as in chevron

READ AND WRITE THE FOLLOWING WORDS:

chaise	chemise	chic	Chopin
chassis	chef	chivalry	
		chiffon	

	chauffeur	chute
		parachute

EXERCISE SENTENCES:

The jeep chassis is by the dock.
Is the jeep chassis by the dock?

The bride rode a chaise to church.
Did the bride ride a chaise to church?

The chef is tasting the chiffon cake.
Is the chef tasting the chiffon cake?

Do chevrons show rank?
Yes, chevrons show rank.

The parachute saved the pilot.
The pilot was saved by the parachute.

You can drop the letter in the mail chute.
Pardon me, your chemise is showing.

USE THE FOLLOWING WORDS IN SENTENCES:

chauffeur	chemise	chef	chute	chevron

THR as in three   3

READ AND WRITE THE FOLLOWING WORDS:

thrash	thread	thrice	throat	thrum
thrasher	threat	thrift	throb	thrush
	thresh	thrill	throne	thrust
	thresher	thrive	throw	

		enthrall		threw
				through

READ THE FOLLOWING SENTENCES:

There is a throbbing pain in his throat.
Is there a throbbing pain in his throat?

Music thrills and enthralls.
Does the music thrill and enthrall?

The thrush, like the thrasher, is a songbird.
Is the thrush a songbird like the thrasher?

Thrice the high jumper tried to clear the bar and failed.
Did the high jumper try to clear the bar thrice and fail?

The threat of global warming is real.
Is the threat of global warming real?

Will you thread the needle for Kate?
Will you give Kate the thread and the needle?

USE THE FOLLOWING WORDS IN SENTENCES:

thrift	throne	throw	through	thrum

LESSON 64
TH as in thistle

READ AND WRITE THE FOLLOWING WORDS:
VOICELESS TH

thank	theater	thick	thong	thud
thatch	thermos	third	thorn	thug
	thief	thing		thump
	thieves	think		thunder

thousand	thaw

VOICED TH

than	the	thine	those	thus
that	thee	this	though	
	their	thy	although	
	them	thyself		
	then			
	thence			
	there			

READ THE FOLLOWING SENTENCES:

Does the thistle have thorns?
No, the thistle has no thorns,
   but it has prickly leaves.

Is the theater closed this winter?
The theater is closed this winter.

You need a thick glass for that window.
That window has a thick glass.

Is thatch roof cool during the summer?
Yes, thatch roof is cool during summer.

Thunder always follows lightning.
Does thunder always follow lightning?

Do you use the thimble on your thumb?
You can use the thimble on your thumb.

The thermos bottle contains hot chocolate.
Does the thermos bottle contain hot chocolate?

Hurricane Hugo renders thousands homeless.
Are thousands rendered homeless
   by Hurricane Hugo?

USE THE FOLLOWING WORDS IN SENTENCES:

thank	thief	thing	think	third

LESSON 65

WH = HW as in whale

READ AND WRITE THE FOLLOWING WORDS:

whack	wheat	while	whorl
wharf	whether	whiff	whopper
what	wheel	whine	
	whet	whim	
	when	whit	
		white	
		why	

WH = H as in whole

who	whoever	whom	whose	whoop
whosoever	whole	wholesale	wholesome	

READ THE FOLLOWING SENTENCES:

Where are you going?
I am going to the wharf today.

While you are at the wharf, will you
buy me some crabs, too?

What will you drive to the the wharf?
I will drive the four wheel drive to the wharf.

Whose white bag is this?
That white bag is mine.

What will you do at the wharf?
I will buy fresh fish at the wharf.

The wheat bread is in the bag.
Is the wheat bread in the bag?

Whale oil was used as fuel before.
Was whale oil used as fuel before?

USE THE FOLLOWING WORDS IN SENTENCES:

whole	wheel	whine	what	whale

PART II

SECTION 6 – Silent Consonants

LESSONS 66-68

LESSON 66 GH = G as in ghost

GN = N as in gnat

READ AND WRITE THE FOLLOWING WORDS:

ghastly	gherkin	ghost
aghast	ghetto	gnome
gnarl		
gnat		
gnash		

gnaw   gnu
                         ghoul

EXERCISE SENTENCES:

The gherkin is a small cucumber.
Is the gherkin a small cucumber?

Ghosts and ghouls exist only in the mind.
Do ghosts and ghouls exist only in the mind?

What is a gnu?
A gnu is a very large antelope.

The gnat is a pesky insect.
Is the gnat a pesky insect?

The trunk of the tree is gnarled.

It is said that a gnome guards a hidden treasure.

The ghetto is a ghastly place.
Is the ghetto a ghastly place?

USE THE FOLLOWING WORDS IN SENTENCES:

ghost   gnat   gherkin   gnash   gnaw

KN = N as in knife

READ AND WRITE THE FOLLOWING WORDS:

knave	knead	knick-knack	knob	knuckle
knack	knee	knight	knock	knew
knapsack	knelt	knit	knoll	
	knell	knives	know	

READ THE FOLLOWING SENTENCES:

Peter's knapsack is full of knick-knacks.
Is Peter's knapsack full of knick-knacks?

The man has a knock-knee.
Does the man have a knock-knee?

Peter, do you know how to tie a bowline knot?
Yes, I know how to tie a bowline knot.

Jim hit his knuckle on the door knob.
Did Jim hit his knuckle on the door knob?

How heavy was a knight's armor?
A knight's armor was very heavy.

"The Man Who Knew Too Much" was a thriller.
Was "The Man Who Knew Too Much" a thriller?

USE THE FOLLOWING WORDS IN SENTENCES:

knife	knead	knock	knee	knit

LESSON 67   PN = N, PT = T, PS = S   RH = R, KH = K

psychic

rhinoceros

READ AND WRITE THE FOLLOWING WORDS:

psalm	pterodactyl	psyche	rhumba
ptarmigan		psychopath	
khaki		psychology	

Psalter

rhubarb
rheumatic
pneumonia

EXERCISE SENTENCES:

The ptarmigan is a grouse.
Is the ptarmigan a grouse.

Pneumonia can be a killer disease.
Is pneumonia a killer disease?

Can a psychic really see the future?
No, even a psychic can not see the future.

The rhubarb pie smells good.
Is that a rhubard pie?

Rhumba is a lively dance.
Is rhumba a lively dance?

A psalm is a sacred song.
Is a psalm a sacred song?

USE THE FOLLOWING WORDS IN SENTENCES:

rhubarb   khaki   psalm   psychic   pneumonia

LESSON 68

SCH = SH and SC = S as in scissors

READ AND WRITE THE FOLLOWING WORDS:

scent	science
scene	scientist
scenery	scion
	scimitar

Schubert
Schumann

READ THE FOLLOWING SENTENCES:

Is it true that lemon scent reduces error?
Yes, test results show that lemon scent does reduce errors.

The war zone is the scene of so much pain and suffering.
Is the war zone the scene of so much pain and suffering?

Schubert and Schumann were composers.
Were Schubert and Schumann composers?

The scimitar is a curved sword used by Arabs.
The curved sword that Arabs use is called a scimitar.

USE THE FOLLOWING WORDS IN SENTENCES:

scissors   scent   science   scientist   scion

WR = R as in write

READ AND WRITE THE FOLLOWING WORDS:

wraith	wreath	writer	wrote	wrung
wrasse	wreck	wriggle	wrong	
wrap	wren	wrinkle		
wrapper	wrench	wrist		

READ THE FOLLOWING SENTENCES:

The wrapper has wrinkles.
Does the wrapper have wrinkles?

Does he write for the local paper?
Yes, he writes for the local paper.

A wraith-like figure was seen near the stairs.
Near the stairs, he saw a wraith-like figure.

He wrote the wrong number.
Did he write the wrong number?

Is the wrasse a spiny fish?
Yes, the wrasse is a spiny fish.

The writer sprained his wrist in the car wreck.
Did the writer sprain his wrist in the car wreck?

USE THE FOLLOWING WORDS IN SENTENCES:

wrap	wrench	wreath	wriggle	wrote

PART II

SECTION 7 – Other Combinations

LESSON 69

LESSON 69
SHR as in shrimp

READ AND WRITE THE FOLLOWING WORDS:

shrank	shred	shrike	shrub
shrapnel	shredded	shrill	shrubbery
	shriek	shrink	shrug
		shrine	shrunk

shroud   shrew

READ THE FOLLOWING SENTENCES:

The shrike is a bird that has a shrill cry.
Does the shrike have a shrill cry.?

A shrapnel shattered his kneecap.
Did a shrapnel shatter his kneecap?

The top of the hill is a nice site for the shrine.
Is the top of the hill a nice site for the shrine?

Shrimps and shredded beef were served for dinner.
Were shrimps and shredded beef served for dinner?

His shrieks can be heard from afar.
Are his shrieks heard from afar?

The shrew is a small mouse-like animal.
The small animal that looks like
   a mouse is a shrew.

USE THE FOLLOWING WORDS IN SENTENCES:

shrink   shrimp   shriek   shrill   shrub

SW as in swan

READ AND WRITE THE FOLLOWING WORDS:

sway	swell	swift	swollen	swung
swab	sweat	swing	swore	
swallow	sweet	swim	sworn	
swat	sweep	swine		

		swarm		swoon
		swamp		swoop

READ THE FOLLOWING SENTENCES:

Huge swells swamp small boats.
Did huge swells swamp small boats?

The flowers are swaying in the breeze.
Are the flowers swaying in the breeze?

A swarm of bees built a hive near the house.
Did a swarm of bees build a hive near the house?

Swollen rivers sweep away homes near river banks.
Did swollen rivers sweep away homes near river banks?

Did the hawk swoop down on the chicks?
Yes, the hawk swooped down on the chicks.

Swans swim in the pond.
Do swans swim in the pond?

The swift and the swallow are both small birds.
Are the swift and the swallow both small birds?

USE THE FOLLOWING WORDS IN SENTENCES:

swab	swallow	sweep	swine	swore

PART III

SECTION 1 – Consonant Blends

as Word Ends

LESSONS 70-75

LESSON 70

EXERCISES: READ THE FOLLOWING WORDS AND SENTENCES

LD as in gold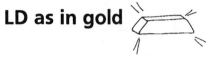

emerald	held	mild	told
herald	weld	wild	cold
Gerald	wield	guild	sold
	yield	build	bold

bald

LGE = LJ as in bulge

indulge
divulge

LC = LK   LK as in milk

talc	elk	silk		bulk
		bilk		hulk
				sulk

LF as in elf

self   golf   gulf

wolf

LM as in elm

helm   film
realm

LP as in gulp

Alps   help

LT as in belt

felt	jilt	jolt	adult
melt	silt	colt	
dealt	wilt	bolt	

salt
halt
fault
vault

LVE = LV as in shelves

valve	elves	resolve
	selves	solve
		dissolve
		involve

wolves

Salt is needed to melt the ice on the road.
Is salt needed to melt the ice on the road?

More runners wilt under the hot sun.
Did more runners wilt under the hot sun?

Is it cold and lonely at the helm?
Yes, it is cold and lonely at the helm.

Many wild animals need help to survive.
Do many wild animals need help to survive?

The colt bolted into the woods.
Did the colt bolt into the woods?

The bulk of the films was exposed.
Was the bulk of the films exposed?

Talc is used to make talcum powder.
Is talc used to make talcum powder?

Does Billy have a mild cold?
Yes, Billy has a mild cold.

USE THE FOLLOWING WORDS IN SENTENCES:

solve	silk	yield	wolf	bald

LESSON 71

EXERCISES: READ THE FOLLOWING WORDS AND SENTENCES

NC = NK   NK as in sink

NX = NKS as in lynx

bank	zinc	honk	bunk
rank	ink	monk	dunk
manx cat	jinx	conk	junk

NCE and NSE = NS as in fence

dance	hence	mince	response	once
lance	tense	since		dunce
	sense	rinse		

pounce
bounce
ounce

ND as in hand

band	fiend	bind	bond
land	bend	find	fond
wand	lend	kind	pond

mound	wound
hound	
round	

NGE = NJ as in sponge

orange	avenge	hinge	lunge
range	revenge	singe	

lounge

NT as in ant

pants	bent	lint	bunt
want	went	mint	hunt
saint	accident	hint	punt
paint	accent	pint	

count	point	taunt
mount	joint	haunt

Billy is fond of junk food.
Is Billy fond of junk food?

Did Bob get a pair of pants for fifty cents?
Bob got a pair of pants for fifty cents.

The bunt is a tactical move in baseball.
Is the bunt a tactical move in baseball?

The response makes a lot of sense.
Did the response make a lot of sense?

The city put a fence by the river bank for safety.
Did the city put a fence by the river bank for safety?

Tom has a bunk bed in his room.
Does Tom have a bunk bed in his room?

Sponge comes from the sea.
Does sponge come from the sea?

The land near the pond is sandy.
Is the land near the pond sandy?

USE THE FOLLOWING WORDS IN SENTENCES;

count   point   hinge   dance   tank

LESSON 72

EXERCISES: READ THE FOLLOWING WORDS AND SENTENCES

RB as in curb

barb wire	herb			disturb
garb	superb		absorb	suburb
	verb			curb

RD as in cards

guard	herd	bird	cord	absurd
ward	beard		hoard	curd
lard	heard		board	

RGE = RJ as in barge

large	merge	forge	urge
Marge	verge	George	purge
		gorge	

RVE = RV as in scarves

carve	nerve		curves
scarves	serve		

RL as in pearl

Carl	earl	girl	whorl	curl
				furl
				hurl

RK as in ark

bark	perk	irk	cork	Turk
dark	jerk	Dirk	fork	lurk
mark		Kirk	work	

RM as in arm

harm	perm	firm	worm
warm			dorm
farm			form

RN as in corn

barn	earn		born	urn
darn	learn		worn	burn
warn	fern		horn	turn

RP as in harp

carp		corpse	burp
warp			slurp

RT as in cart

mart	Bert	dirt	abort	curt
part	pert		export	hurt
art			extort	

court

RSE and RCE = RS as in horse

farce	coerce	pierce	coarse	curse
	universe	fierce	hoarse	purse
	disperse		worse	

course

Do not burn leaves near the barn.
Did you burn leaves near the barn?

Dirk has a hoarse voice.
Does Dirk have a hoarse voice?

The curt reply hurt Tom.
Did the curt reply hurt Tom?

The girl's hair had curls.
Did the girl's hair have curls?

Some medicines come from herbs.
Do some medicines come from herbs?

Don jerked the cork out of the bottle.
Did Don jerk the cork out of the bottle?

The barb wire keeps the herd of
cattle fenced in.
Does the barb wire keep the herd
of cattle fenced in?

Birds and worms do a lot of harm to the farm.
Do birds and worms do a lot of harm to the farm?

USE THE FOLLOWING WORDS IN SENTENCES:

absorb	large	serve	girl	learn

LESSON 73

EXERCISES: READ THE FOLLOWING WORDS AND SENTENCES

SK as in mask

cask	desk	disk	husk
bask		risk	tusk
task			

SM as in prism

sarcasm	chrism	Communism
chasm	baptism	

SP as in wasp

asp	lisp
hasp	wisp
rasp	

ST as in nest

cast	best	fist	cost	dust
past	rest	mist	post	must
fast	west	list	most	burst
last	test	cyst	coast	
			boast	

oust	hoist		boost
	moist		roost

STE = ST = as in paste

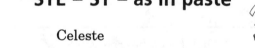

taste	Celeste
haste	
waste	

Sarcasm is biting wit.
Is sarcasm biting wit?

The task is not without risks.
Is the task not without risks?

She is a wisp of a girl.
Is she a wisp of a girl?

Chrism is holy oil used in baptism.
Is Chrism holy oil used in baptism?

Tom needs cash to buy a face mask.
Does Tom need cash to buy a face mask?

The disk is on top of the desk.
Is the disk on top of the desk?

The saying, "Haste makes waste," makes sense.
Does the saying, "Haste makes waste," make sense?

The first and last man to hold the post was Tom.
Was Tom the first and last man to hold the post?

USE THE FOLLOWING WORDS IN SENTENCES:

waste	test	coast	dust	baptism

LESSON 74

EXERCISES: READ THE FOLLOWING WORDS AND SENTENCES

BLE = B'L as in table

cable	feeble	nibble	cobble	humble
able	pebble	bible	noble	bubble
amble			hobble	mumble

audible

CLE = K'L and
CKLE = K'L as in pickle

tackle	fickle	suckle
cackle	pickle	buckle
hackle	cycle	uncle

DLE = D'L as in candle

saddle	peddle	idle	fondle	bundle
paddle	meddle	fiddle	coddle	muddle
				noodle
				poodle

FLE = F'L as in waffle

raffle	rifle	ruffle
baffle		muffle

GLE = G'L as in eagle

dangle	beagle	jingle	goggle	juggle
mangle		giggle	ogle	bungle
tangle		single		jungle

PLE = P'L as in apple

sample	people	simple	topple	purple
maple		dimple		supple
		pimple		rumple

SCLE = S'L and
STLE = S'L as in whistle

castle	nestle	thistle	jostle	muscle
	pestle			rustle
				hustle

TLE = T'L as in bottle

battle	beetle	little	mottle	cuttle fish
rattle	nettle	title		
cattle	mettle			

ZLE = Z'L as in puzzle

| dazzle | | fizzle | nozzle | guzzle |
| | | sizzle | | muzzle |

Cuttle fish is a delicacy for some people.
Is cuttle fish a delicacy for some people?

Little beetles eat the apple seeds.
Did little beetles eat the apple seeds?

There is a big bundle of hay for cattle feed.
Is there a big bundle of hay for cattle feed?

Sam had a fiddle, a bugle, and a whistle.
Does Sam have a fiddle, a bugle and a whistle?

The pickled dills are in a couple of bottles.
Are the pickled dills in a couple of bottles?

The castle nestles by the side of the hill.
Does the castle nestle by the side of the hill?

Have many people read the Bible?
Many people have read the bible.

Simple people have simple needs.
Do simple people have simple needs?

Some people do not like the hustle and bustle of city life.
Do some people not like the hustle and bustle of city life?

USE THE FOLLOWING WORDS IN SENTENCES:

| dimple | pimple | bubble | single | buckle |

LESSON 75

EXERCISES: READ THE FOLLOWING WORDS AND SENTENCES:

CT = KT as in convict

act	defect	distinct	conduct
fact	elect	extinct	deduct
impact	eject		

FT as in gift

raft	left	lift	loft	tuft
		rift	soft	
		sift		

PT as in erupt

apt	wept	script	opt	abrupt
adapt	kept	Egypt	adopt	disrupt
rapt		crypt		

MP as in lamp

camp	empty	limp	romp	bump
damp	hemp	pimp		dump
ramp	tempt	wimp		pump

The giant auk is extinct.
Is the giant auk extinct?

The pump has a defect in the seal.
Does the pump have a defect in the seal?

Are all the gifts in the loft?
Yes, all the gifts are in the loft.

The camp is empty at this time of the year.
Is the camp empty at this time of the year?

The script was adapted from a novel.
Was the script adapted from a novel?

The convict hid in the dump site for days.
Did the convict hide in the dump site for days?

The city elects a mayor today.
Does the city elect elect a mayor today?

Is it a fact that bad diet is harmful to health?
It is a fact that bad diet is harmful to health.

USE THE FOLLOWING WORDS IN SENTENCES:

raft	left	soft	bump	deduct

PART III

SECTION 2 – Digraphs as Word Ends

LESSONS 76-77

LESSON 76

EXERCISES: READ THE FOLLOWING WORDS AND SENTENCES:

CH as in peach

beach	coach	touch
reach	poach	much
teach	roach	such

LCH

belch	milch cow	mulch

NCH

ranch	bench	pinch	bunch
	quench	lynch	lunch

RCH

arch	perch	birch	torch	lurch
march	search		porch	

TCH

patch	etch	ditch	botch	Dutch
watch	fetch	pitch	notch	hutch

pouch   launch

CK = K as in duck

back	neck	lick	lock	tuck
pack	peck	pick	rock	puck

DGE = DJ as in judge

badge	ledge	midge	dodge	budge
	edge	ridge	lodge	nudge

PH = F as in autograph

epitaph	telephone
seraph	

The man was rough and tough.
Was the man rough and tough?

In summer, every inch of the beach
    is covered with birds.
Is every inch of the beach covered
    with birds in summer?

Are robins perched on the porch?
Yes, robins are perched on the porch.

The torch parade marched under the arch.
Did the torch parade march under the arch?

A damp match will not catch fire.
Will a damp match catch fire?

Do ducks fly south in the winter?
Yes, ducks fly south in the winter.

Milch cows supply the ranch with milk.
Do milch cows supply the ranch with milk?

A pinch of salt will make your lunch taste better.
Will a pinch of salt make your lunch taste better?

Mulch will help the soil retain water.
Will mulch help the soil retain water?

USE THE FOLLOWING WORDS IN SENTENCES:

teach   bench   torch   edge   laugh

LESSON 77

EXERCISES: READ THE FOLLOWING WORDS AND SENTENCES:

NG as in wings

rang	king	among	hung
gang	ring	song	lung
bang	sing	long	

SH as in cash

dash	leash	dish	hush
wash	mesh	fish	rush

LSH

Walsh

RSH

marsh
harsh

bush

TH as in tooth

bath	teeth	myth	month	Ruth
math	beneath		moth	Duluth
bathe	death		loathe	

DTH

width

PTH

depth

LTH

health	filth
wealth	

RTH

hearth	birth	north
earth		fourth

mouth	sooth
south	booth

You need cash to buy fish.
Do you need cash to buy fish?

Ruth sings the song best.
Does Ruth sing the song best?

Wash the dishes before you go out.
Did you wash the dishes before you went out?

"Fire! Fire!" and the dash for the exits followed.
Did the dash for the exits follow, "Fire! Fire!"?

Did you measure the length and width of the table?
Yes, I measured the length and width of the table.

High medical costs give new meaning to "Health is wealth."
Does high medical cost give new meaning to "Health is wealth"?

Math is not an easy subject.
Is Math an easy subject?

The king is out on a fox hunt.
Is the king out on a fox hunt?

Is the fourth of the month a holiday?
Yes, the fourth of the month is a holiday.

"Sing a Song of Sixpence" is a nursery song.
Is "Sing a Song of Sixpence" a nursery song?

USE THE FOLLOWING WORDS IN SENTENCES:

wash   dish   beneath   mouth   teeth

PART III

SECTION 3 – Silent Consonants

LESSON 78-79

LESSON 78

EXERCISES: READ THE FOLLOWING WORDS AND SENTENCES:

BT = T as in debt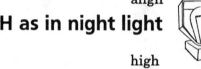

doubt

GM = M and GN = N as in sign

campaign	phlegm	assign	bologna
reign		design	
lasagna		resign	
		align	

GH as in night light

weight	high	dough	Hugh
neigh	sight		Pugh
neighbor	sigh		
weigh	might		
	height		
	right		

---

bough	fought
	caught
	taught
	naughty
	daughter

LF = F, LK = K, LM = M and LVE = V as in calf

half	folk
balm	holm oak
calm	
halve	

---

caulk
talk
balk
walk

MB = M and MN = M as in comb

jamb	condemn	limb	bomb	dumb
lamb	solemn	hymn		numb
damn				column

---

autumn	tomb
	womb

SC = S and
ST = S as in castle

hasten	pestle	listen	muscle
fasten	nestle		bustle
			rustle

moisten

The highlight of the event was the mile race.
Was the mile race the highlight of the event?

Hugh likes doughnuts and bologna.
Does Hugh like doughnuts and bologna?

To escape, the convict sought the cover of night.
The convict sought the cover of night to escape.

Is the kite caught in the holm oak?
Yes, the kite is caught in the holm oak.

To escape, the convict sought the cover of night.
The convict sought the cover of night to escape.

The neon light sign does not weigh much.
Does the neon light sign weigh much?

The huge quake damage numbs the folks.
The folks are numbed by the huge quake
  damage.

Does Bob doubt if he can pay his debt today?
Yes, Bob doubts if he can pay his debt today.

The campaign to save rain forests gains support.
Did the campaign to save rain forests gain support?

USE THE FOLLOWING WORDS IN SENTENCES:

calm   walk   lamb   autumn   fasten

LESSON 79   OTHER SILENT CONSONANTS

READ THE FOLLOWING WORDS AND SENTENCES:

sandwich	often	myrrh	mortgage	cupboard
yacht	soften	isle	depot	debut
Mardi Gras	answer	islet	sword	
handsome	receipt	island	two	
grandma	Wednesday	aisle	almond	
grandpa	salmon	debris	asthma	

	Iroquois	Arkansas	could	Sioux
	Illinois		would	rendezvous
			should	

They will rendezvous on an island.
Will they rendezvous on an island?

Hurricane Hugo left tons of debris.
Did Hurricane Hugo leave tons of debris?

One day, the boy could be king.
The boy could be a king one day.

Asthma often bothers him.
Does asthma often bother him?

Grandma and grandpa love salmon.
Do grandma and grandpa love salmon?

Could it be the answer to the puzzle?
Yes, it could be the answer to the puzzle.

USE THE FOLLOWING WORDS IN SENTENCES:

handsome	Mardi Gras	sword	cupboard	yacht

PART III

SECTION 4 – Other Word Ends

LESSONS 80-81

LESSON 80

EXERCISES: READ THE FOLLOWING WORDS AND SENTENCES

(S)CIOUS and TIOUS = SHUS as in delicious

malicious	vicious	conscious	luscious
anxious	ambitious	obnoxious	

cautious	superstitious

CIAL and TIAL = SHUL as in martial arts

partial	essential	initial	social
impartial			

SION and TION = SHUN as in mansion

action	session	vision	lotion	junction
passion	petition	addition	motion	question
	mention	mission		solution

audition
auction

CEAN, CIAN, TIAN and SIAN = SHUN as in musician

Asian	Venetian	politician	Russian
Martian		ocean	

CIE, SIE and TIE = SHU as in patient

ancient	efficient	conscience	quotient	sufficient
patience			

TU = CHOO as in perceptual

actual	eventual	virtue	mutual
factual	perpetual		punctual
habitual			

TURE = CHER
as in picture

nature	gesture	mixture	posture	future
pasture	adventure		torture	suture
mature				puncture

moisture

S = ZH as in treasure

casual	leisure	vision	usury
casualty	measure	television	usurer
		artesian well	usual
			visual

Russian art is on exhibit.
Is Russian art on exhibit?

There is no action yet on the petition.
Is there action on the petition yet?

Passions ran high at the last council session.
Did passions run high at the last council
  session?

There is treasure beneath the ocean.
Beneath the ocean there is treasure.

Ripe mangoes are luscious.
Are ripe mangoes luscious?

Dance is music in motion.
Is dance music in motion?

No one knows what the actual damage is.
Does anyone know what the actual damage is?

Tom is a good addition to the team.
Is Tom a good addition to the team?

USE THE FOLLOWING WORDS IN SENTENCES:

picture   measure   punctual   conscious   solution

LESSON 81

EXERCISES — READ THE FOLLOWING WORDS AND SENTENCES:

OUS = US
as in curious

famous   nervous   vigorous   obvious   furious

ION = YUN as in onion

hellion   million   dominion   union
medallion   billion

ACE and ICE = IS
as in edifice

malice   Venice   notice   surface
Alice   menace   office   prejudice
Candace   furnace

ILE = IL as in textile

agile   fertile   imbecile   futile
                                  missile

INE = IN
as in machine

masculine   examine   imagine   iodine   urine
gasoline   determine   cuisine
famine   engine
                 medicine

ATE and ITE = IT
as in chocolate

agate   senate   infinite   opposite   accurate
                 definite   minute   duplicate
                 delicate   immediate
                 separate

IVE = IV as in olive

active   sensitive   give   motive
passive   negative   live   positive
massive   sedative   submissive   possessive
native   extensive
attentive

GUE = G
as in tongue

vague

league
colleague
Decalogue

intrigue

dialogue
rogue
monologue

AGE, EGE and
IGE=IJ as baggage

garbage
damage
manage
passage
package
language
bandage

message

image
village
privilege

college
hostage
mortgage
cottage
bondage

luggage
courage

coinage

sausage

The mechanic needs to examine the engine.
Does the mechanic need to examine the engine?

Massive food aid is needed to combat famine.
To combat famine, massive food aid is needed.

The hospital needs essential medicine
  to fight the epidemic.
Does the hospital need essential medicine
  to fight the epidemic?

Did the fireman examine the office for a gas leak?
Yes, the fireman examined the office for a gas leak.

Is patience one of his virtues?
No, patience is not one of his virtues.

Are the sausages expensive?
Yes, the sausages are expensive.

Is the story factual and accurate?
Yes, the story is factual and accurate.

The land near the volcano is fertile.
Is the land near the volcano fertile?

USE THE FOLLOWING WORDS IN SENTENCES:

cottage   luggage   vague   message   package

PART III

SECTION 5 – Unusual Word Ends

LESSON 82

LESSON 82

UNUSUAL ENDINGS: READ THE FOLLOWING WORDS AND SENTENCES

ballet	genie	cachalot	debut
E, EE, ET as long A	**IE, E** as long E	**EAU, OT** as long O	**UT** as long U

EXERCISE WORDS:

ballet	genie	depot	debut
valet	recipe	bureau	
parquet	calorie	Costeau	
fillet	Annie	plateau	
bouquet	Debbie	potpourri	
buffet	Angie	Bordeaux	
Monet	Laramie		
ricochet	laddie		
cafe	cowrie		
matinee	Apache		
toupee	Comanche		
resume			

escritoire	garage
OIR = WAR	**GE = ZH**

abattoir	beige
reservoir	rouge
memoir	mirage
repertoire	entourage
	barrage
	corsage

What is an escritoire?

An escritoire is a writing desk.

The bullet ricocheted and hit him in the arm.
Did the bullet ricochet and hit him in the arm?

Costeau and his colleagues have studied
  the oceans for years.
Have Costeau and his colleagues studied
  the oceans for years?

The water level at the reservoir is low.
Is the water level at the reservoir low?

Jazz music is in his repertoire.
Is jazz music in his repertoire?

Was his debut a success?
Yes, his debut was a success.

Did he order a fish fillet sandwich for lunch?
He ordered a fish fillet sandwich for lunch.

The garage needs repairs.
Can you repair the garage door?

USE THE FOLLOWING WORDS IN SENTENCES:

ballet	resume	depot	mirage	corsage

PART IV

PRACTICE READING MATERIALS

THE VALUE OF READING

A man in his late years leans on a fence by the river. Suddenly the fence gives way. He falls into the river. The river is deep and he cannot swim. Luckily for him, someone is there to pull him out of the river — a real lifesaver. Why did this accident happen? It happened because the man cannot read. There was a big sign on the fence. It read: "DANGER: DO NOT LEAN ON THE FENCE."

A building foreman gets hit by a falling piece of wood. He is lucky to be wearing his safety helmet. He suffers minor injuries, nothing more. Why did the foreman venture into a danger zone? It turned out the foreman could not read. "KEEP OUT: FALLING DEBRIS," the sign clearly said.

Some accidents happen because some people cannot read. They cannot read warning signs on the road. They cannot read warning signs in picnic areas and other sites. They cannot read warning labels on cans and bottles that contain toxic matter. They cannot read simple directions. Because of this, they are always in danger of getting into bad situations. Bad situations may not be life or death situations. The bad situation may be related to a person's job. It may relate to the manner in which the person sees himself. Or, it may relate to the way a person sees the world around him.

How many persons cannot move up the job ladder because they cannot read. Unless they can, these persons cannot get out of the room at the bottom. The job cellar becomes a prison from which there is no escape for them. It is not easy to be in the job cellar. But one does not have to reside in the cellar forever. The ability to read offers a way out of that cellar.

Just as the ability to read offers a way out of the job cellar, it also offers a new way of looking at oneself. The person who cannot read feels he has less wit than the person who can. While this is not necessarily true, the non-reader cannot help but have low self esteem. He feels less confident than the person who can read. At times he feels helpless and lost.

Learning to read is not more difficult than learning any other skill, like riding a bike. To learn to read, one learns to identify the letters of the alphabet. Then he masters the sounds that are associated with these letters, whether the letters are alone or in tandem. After he learns these sounds by heart he is ready to take the next logical step, and that is to practice reading words, sentences and paragraphs. The only way to become a good reader is to keep on reading. That is the same way with riding a bike. To be a better rider, one must keep riding a bike.

If you say, "But learning to read is not that simple," then think of this. We learn thousands upon thousands of words, such as cups, bike, fish, dog, pole, read, meal, leg, take, make and rose. We associate them with objects or actions. We use them properly in sentences. We are understood by others when we use words. We understand others when they use words. Is it really that difficult to learn 26 letters of the alphabet? How difficult is it to associate these letters, alone or in tandem, with 45 sounds they make? If one can master and use thousands of words and attach them to their objects, I reckon it will not be difficult to master 26 letters and 45 sounds.

Having learned to read, we become free. We step out of the shadow of self doubt and lack of confidence. At last, we have a tool with which to master our ignorance and gain new insights. We feel better. We can conquer tedium and boredom. We become more aware, more alive. We enjoy life in a manner we have not done before. Reading has delivered us to a new and exciting world.

OF HABITS, GOOD OR BAD

Man is made of flesh and blood, and more. Man is also a bundle of good and bad habits. A bundle of bad habits means a bundle of dollars down the drain. Indeed, bad habits are costly. Good habits rarely cost much. In the long run, they save a bundle. Exercise is a good habit that does not cost a dime. You can exercise without even getting out of the house. Jogging in place is a good way to keep fit. Come rain or snow, you can always jog in place in your house. Exercise can save several visits to the doctor. The doctor is one person you do not like to visit often. The doctor may be nice, but his fees can be a burden. Regular exercise keeps you away from the doctor and can keep you alive and well longer.

Reading is one more good habit that you can cultivate. There is danger in an idle hour. Idleness can cause boredom; boredom can be the cause of mischief. Reading keeps you out of mischief while it informs, amuses and widens your horizons. A good book is really like a good friend — maybe a tad better. It is honest and will tell you no lies. It consoles and offers sage advice. It tells jokes when you need them. Heaven knows how many times we need such useful diversions. Like a good friend, a good book is always there for you.

Among man's bad habits, I would rate idleness, alcohol, and cigarettes as among the worst. Alcohol and cigarettes cause cancer and many other diseases. Alcohol is a drug. It lessens the power of reason and self-control. It leads to bad judgment, wasted man-hours, and poor workmanship. It lessens self-respect.

A cigarette burns your lungs as surely as it burns a hole in your pocket. Cigarette smoke affects the non-smokers who are around the smoker. Cancer is not choosy. It will afflict the direct, as well as the indirect user of cigarettes. What is bad is that you can obtain alcohol and cigarettes as easily as you can get a soda pop or a bubble gum.

There is nothing worse than the idle hour. The idle hour is an evil hour, for many reasons. It is the hour when the evil genie stirs and leads man to many senseless, mindless crimes and vices. Even when idleness does not lead to anything more than a wasted hour, it is still harmful. We seldom think of time as a limited commodity because we seem to have plenty of it. Yet, of all the things we can dispose of, time is the most limited. We only have 24 hours a day, not a second more. A second lost is lost forever. Time, unlike any other commodity, cannot be replaced or renewed. For those who have not learned to value a second, a basketball game will enlighten. Victory or defeat hangs in a second. A second is all the losing team may need, and does not get.

Life is a game of sorts. How well you manage those fleeting seconds is the margin between success or failure. We cannot be busy all the time, but by filling the vacant hour with a useful hobby, such as reading, we can keep the demons of idleness at bay. Mental exercise like reading can be tough. It drains the body as well. Exercise regularly, and there is no problem. If jogging does not suit you, walking briskly is just as good.

THE COCONUT: A SUPER, SUPER MARKET

Unless you live in an area where coconuts abound, you will never realize how truly amazing the coconut is. Of all the trees (yes, it is a tree), there is none with more uses than the coconut tree. More than eight hundred products are obtained from the coconut palm. Indeed, the coconut is a super, super market.

The bamboo? Yes, it rivals the coconut in number of uses, but the bamboo is not a tree. It is a grass, though it is, indeed, a giant grass.

The coconut's usefulness begins by simply being where it is. Its long, thick roots hold the soil very well. The soil erodes less. Another plus: coconut trees, with leaves twenty feet long, have to be planted far from each other. This permits planting of vegetables, root crops, or even coffee in the wide spaces between them.

Let us take the leaves. The leaves can be bundled together to make a roof. A hut with a roof made of coconut leaves is cool, even on hot, summer days. If you can make a roof out of the leaves, surely you can make a hat or a basket, too. The ribs of the leaves can be used as rafters for the hut.

The coconut flower, when cut, gives out a sweet sap called toddy. Drunk fresh, it is a rich, refreshing drink. Allowed to ferment, it turns into a kind of arrack, a liquor. It can make you tipsy or even get you drunk. (Beware getting drunk. You can get a big headache.) You can also make vinegar out of toddy. Before the flower opens, you may cut the bud out and make a good tasting salad out of it. The bud is called palm cabbage.

The fruit (nut) gives us a number of useful things. Let us begin with the husk. The husk gives us coir, a kind of fiber. This fiber is made into doormats, placemats, belts, ropes, baskets, brooms and brushes. When the fiber is rubberized, it makes good mattresses. The coco dust is used to enrich garden soil. Any woody part of the coconut tree can be used as firewood.

The coconut shell has many uses, also. You can make buttons, cups and beads, and you can use them as inlays on furniture and crafts. The hard shell is an efficient fuel. The charcoal from the burned shells soaks up toxic fumes and gases very well. Coconut charcoal can also be used to soak up bad odors and foul smells.

Inside the shell is the coconut meat and a colorless liquid, which is a natural cool aid. There is nothing like this liquid to cool and refresh you on a hot summer day. This is what is called the coconut milk. Someone should try to bottle the milk.

The coconut meat is a variety store. The meat is food in itself, but it can be used to make cakes, pies, cookies, candy or jams. When the meat is dried, the product is copra. From the copra comes coconut oil. Coconut oil has been used as food for thousands of years. Today, it is used to make soap, butter substitutes, cosmetics, and other items. The oil is obtained when copra is pressed. The leftover meat is made into a cattle feed called coconut cake.

From the stem of the coconut tree comes cabinet wood and porcupine wood. Imelda Marcos built houses made mostly of coconut wood to showcase its use as lumber. Coconut stems are so sturdy that during the Pacific War, they were used as posts and supports for bridges. A coconut tree can live from seventy-five to one hundred years, a long period of quality service.

You see, the coconut is not just a super, super market. It is truly a wonder tree.

(Sources: "Coconut," *Encyclopedia Britannica*, 1973 ed., Vol. 6; "Coconut," *Young People's Science Encyclopedia*, 3rd printing, 1962.)

SOYBEAN, THE ULTIMATE HEALTH FOOD

What is the ultimate health food? Is it lean meat, fish or poultry? The answer is: "none of the above." The ultimate health food is the soybean. If the coconut is a super, super market, the soybean is a convenience store and houseware store combined. You can say it is in the office supply business, too. It may not have as many uses as the coconut, but as a health food it has no equal.

The soybean, like peas and lentils, is a member of the legume family. The peanut, as you might have thought, is a pea. The soybean has pods which contain seeds. That is why it is a legume. It does well on fertile, sandy loams, but it succeeds in almost any type of soil. Some hardy types resist the pod borer, an insect pest. The borer is one of the soybean's natural enemies.

In Asia, the soybean is valued for its seed. The seed is used for a variety of food stuffs. Let us visit a supermarket and find out if we can identify and buy some. Tofu, a bean curd, is a soybean product. Tofu figures in many Asian menus; you can fry it in cooking oil. After it is fried, you can dip it in soy sauce. The cooking oil and soy sauce are likely to be made from soybeans. Some salad oils are made from soybeans. Even macaroni has soybeans in it. With luck, we can find candied beans for dessert. Candied beans are made by boiling beans in syrup.

If you read the labels with care, you may find soybeans in cakes, cookies, sausages and other meat products. In meat products, like sausages, it is used as a binder.

You relax. You are on your sun deck. You sip your beer, savoring its taste. You wonder why this beer tastes better than the one you had a week before. Maybe, just maybe, the yeast used in making it was grown in soybean meal. The meal is what is left after oil is pressed out of the bean. It is used not only in beer-making. The meal is rich in protein; it is used as livestock and poultry feed.

Soybean oil is also widely used. It is in the enamel coating in your washer, dryer, and car. It is in the paint in your room, the varnish in your cabinets, the ink in your pens, the sealant in your bathroom, and the linoleum in your kitchen. It glues together your plywood wall. It is a filler and binder in the paper you use. It makes the fire foam in your fire extinguisher stable. It may be in a woman's cosmetics.

It's such a little bean, but it takes care of more than just your health.

(Source: "Soybean," *Encyclopedia Britannica*, 1973 ed., Vol. 20 on Soybean.)

POTATO, ANYONE?

Idaho is to potato as Virginia is to tobacco and as Florida is to tomato. The common aspect of Idaho, Virginia, and Florida is that they are all states of the United States of America. What is the common aspect of potato, tomato, and tobacco? They are all members of the same family. Yes sir, they are! They are members of the nightshade family. It is ironic that the tomato was once deemed poisonous, but people were inhaling an insidious poison in tobacco smoke. They were chewing tobacco, too!

The potato is a tuber, which means that it does not grow from a seed. It grows from pieces of the tuber which have "eyes." The "eye" is a bud which is not yet developed. Did you ever leave a potato for some time? A bud grows out of the "eye," and your salad must wait for the next potato harvest.

Like the soybean and the coconut, the potato is highly valued as food. When the potato crop failed in Ireland in 1846, many people died of famine. Like the coconut and the soybean, the potato has many natural enemies. Virus, fungus, rot, bugs, and insects like the leaf hopper kill it. The potato bug kills it by eating its leaves. However, the potato is every bit as hardy as the bean and the coconut. It seems that disease and bugs cannot keep it away from super markets.

It comes raw in netted bags or as chips and other food stuffs in labeled bags, boxes, and cans. What about the popular "French fries," which may not even be French, but Irish? No fast food diner can do without it. To teenagers, food is "French fries" and soda.

At home, the potato salad is a rich, quick meal. It is quite easy to make. It does not take culinary genius to make it. Peel off five good sized potatoes, boil and dice; chop a stalk of celery, slice a hard boiled egg; put them in a bowl, add mayonnaise, mustard, salt, and pepper. Mix them and you have a hearty meal. Pardon me? If it does not look like potato salad that is because I am not a chef. That is how I do it, though, and believe me, it tastes good.

(Source: "Potato," "Potato Bug" and "Tomato," *Britannica Junior Encyclopedia*, 1972 ed.)

AIDS: A KILLER DISEASE

Not so long ago "aids" was a harmless verb which meant "helps." It was a good turn you could do for someone. A virus has changed that, and today, "AIDS" has taken a new and sinister meaning. It is a disease which someone may give you. It has no cure. The donor may not even know that he has become a messenger of agony and death.

Like sonar or radar, "AIDS" is an acronym. It stands for the first letters of the name *Acquired Immune Deficiency Syndrome*. Unlike sonar or radar, which are useful tools, "AIDS" is a killer. It is caused by a virus which attacks the human immune system. The immune system weakens and the victim easily succumbs to diseases. AIDS is transmitted through sex or exchange of blood in transfusions or through open wounds. Among drug addicts, it is transmitted by common use of needles. The disease can remain undetected for as long as ten years. This is likely the reason why many are infected with "AIDS" today. Without knowing it, a person can carry and transmit it to others for years.

A spot of common house bleach kills the virus on contact. Once inside the body, however, there is no known medicine that can kill it. Medical men are trying hard to find a drug that can combat it. So far they have not come up with one that can. The AZT drug inhibits the virus from multiplying. But it is not a cure. A vaccine has been tried. Those who got the vaccine developed "AIDS" antibodies. It is not known if the antibodies will work against live "AIDS" virus.

Some doctors see natural hormones as a source of hope. These natural hormones boost the immune system. Doctors hope that the hormones can be developed to fight not only "AIDS," but also cancer, anemia, and other diseases.

What is the best way to fight the virus at this time? For laymen like us, the best way to fight the virus is to avoid it. Yes, avoid it. That means no drugs, no exchange of needles. That means safe sex. Will condoms make sex safe? Maybe. Some condoms have tested porous. They are unsafe. Thus, the only safe sex is sex with one's spouse.

But I may get it from my dentist or my doctor. Now that I think of it, I see that this is another problem.

(Sources: *Discover*, Jan '88, Feb '88, and Sep '87.)

OF CYCLONES, VOLCANOES, AND QUAKES

We do not have dominion over all, but we are masters of many. We have reasons to feel ten feet tall, safe, and secure, but we have reasons, also, to fear the future. We have landed men on the moon. With robot eyes, we have seen the terrain of Mars and Venus and discovered alien moons. We explore the ocean depths and put huge space stations and telescopes into orbit. In many cases, we have conquered disease. We suffer hunger, but not much. There is poverty, but living conditions are improving. There is despair, but there is also hope. The world in general seems to be changing for better.

For better or for worse, we have harnessed the awesome power of the atom. We use this power to produce energy. We also use the same power to threaten mass murder. Nuclear accidents happen. Our best efforts to avoid them seem fruitless. Think of Three Mile Island and Chernobyl. Both have a message. While the atom serves us, we are not its master. Its awesome power is like a genie: it can be good; it can be evil.

Like the power of the atom, there are others we cannot hope to tame. Recently, two volcanoes blew their tops in the Pacific and poured out tons of lava, mud, and ash. There is nothing we can do about it. One quake, then another, shook up California badly. The killer quake is still fresh in our minds. Every now and then we are told that a cyclone leaves many dead and many more homeless. The fury of a cyclone is terrible to behold. The biggest bombs ever built are mere firecrackers compared to a cyclone. Yearly, the Bay of Bengal, off the Indian sub-continent, gets this unwelcome visit. We tremble. We wait for the next unwelcome visit. It will come. We are not able to prevent it.

Surely, the rain comes down. How much or how little, we cannot foretell. If it rains too much, there is flood. If it rains too little, the soil is too dry for sowing. Either way we suffer. Winter too, comes and goes. We cannot tell how severe the coming winters will be. A severe winter is always a misery. It comes every now and then, heedless and unrelenting. Like floodwaters, deep snow holds everything to a standstill.

Nature's power may be awesome, but it is not what we must fear most. Nature has visited and revisited us with its most awesome forces: disease, famine, volcanic eruptions, quakes and cyclones. We are still here, teeming in our millions and billions. This puny being is not so puny after all.

Where Nature has failed, we might succeed. Nature cannot get rid of us, but we may yet get rid of ourselves and everything else. We may nuke ourselves to oblivion. Is it a comfort that the big powers are reducing their nuclear weapons? It is a fool who thinks that the world is safer because of it. The big powers have enough left to blow up the planet many times over, yet that is not where lies the greatest danger. Big powers weigh their options carefully. The leaders reason and think. They are not likely to pull the nuclear trigger that easily. The danger lies elsewhere.

Small nations and small men want to feel big. They are crazy enough to try to acquire nuclear weapons because it gives them the feel of power. Saddam Hussein seems to be on the verge of success. He may be a small step away from putting a big bomb together. When he does, there is no telling what he may do with it. His acts defy logic and reason. They border on madness. That is why he is a very dangerous man. How many Saddams are there in the world? No exact count could be made. Even if Saddam is unique, there is always an Idi Amin waiting in the wings to take center stage. An Idi is every bit as evil and harmful as a Saddam.

Idi and Saddam picture the beast in us. Both write a bloody tale of torture, murder, war, violence, greed, and hate. Peace is but a respite between periods of anger, hate, and despair. Why does stable peace elude us? Is it because, as some say, war and violence is a legacy of our animal nature? If so, are we doomed to follow the beast and not the best in us? Are we slaves of instinct or masters of our fate?

Men of peace and goodwill have come and gone. Their lives tell us that we can attain peace. We can free ourselves from fear. We can feel safe and secure. But first we must tame the beast in us. We can only be masters of our fate if we follow the path of peace. If we must shake in anger, blow our tops or vent our fury, if we must make war, then let it be against greed, injustice, prejudice, drugs, poverty, ignorance, bigotry, violence, and hate.

CARE FOR THE LAND, THE AIR AND THE SEA, OR DIE

We no longer see land as limitless. Cities, towns, and villages dot hills, mountainsides, beaches, riversides, and valleys. Man is everywhere. Even in once forbidding rain forests, teeming humanity has come and conquered its environs. In doing so, man, the maker and user of tools, has put a heavy burden on land.

The soil gives man life and nurture. To meet basic food, fuel, housing, medical, water and sanitary needs, man unduly burdens the soil. To get rid of bugs and other insects and be assured of a good harvest, man uses a number of toxic killers. Man denudes huge areas of forest lands. He needs lumber for housing and furniture, or simply wood for firewood. He needs land to raise his livestock, grow his rice, soybean, wheat, rye and fruit. He gouges hills and mountains for metal ores and minerals and leaves gaping wounds on their sides. When rain comes, the rich top soil erodes. The top soil erodes because the forest which soaks up the rain water is gone. The roots which hold the soil are gone, too. The top soil becomes useless mud deposits at the bottom of lakes, ponds and rivers. Rivers carry some of this mud to the sea where it suffocates and kills off coral reefs. Coral reefs are rich feeding and spawning grounds for sea life. The sea is one of man's main sources of food and medicine.

This is not the only way man harms land and sea. He dumps waste into landfills (or directly into the sea). Some are toxic. Asbestos, mercury, lead, bug killers and acids are but a few of the toxins. Some, like nuclear waste, emit deadly rays. They kill land and sea animals. They harm man, too. Toxic waste can seep into aquifers (underground, fresh water deposits). If it does, water becomes unsafe for human or animal use.

Oil spills are another threat to the safety of the seas and the life they support. In Alaska, there was an enormous oil spill which spoiled miles and miles of beaches, killed fish, aquatic birds, and marine plants. There are other less known but equally lethal spills.

Even the air we inhale may not be safe anymore. We pollute the air as surely as we pollute land and sea. Daily, we send up into the air tons and tons of waste from our cars, our homes, and our factories. Recently a senseless man called Saddam burned oil fields in Kuwait. Many of the fields are still burning, further polluting the air.

What goes up must come down, so the saying goes. The waste we send up comes down. It comes down as acid rain to do more damage to forests, lakes, rivers, and seas. Already, man is reaping what he has sown. He is being paid back for his lack of care with such woes as cancer, polluted waters, diseased fish and fowl, lead and mercury poisoning and a hole in the ozone layer above the earth.

We must not forget that we are part of one ecological system. The harm we do to the system is the harm we do to ourselves. We must care, or die with the system.

DRUNK DRIVER, THE HIDDEN MENACE ON THE ROAD

A seven-year-old boy boards the bus. Like other boys already in the bus, he looks forward to a whole day of fun at the zoo. This is not his first visit to the zoo. Like the rest of the boys, he knows that it is fun to have a picnic at the zoo. He waves goodbye to his mom and dad. He is happy and full of life. Soon, he and some other boys on the bus will be dead. There is a menace on the bus; the driver is a drunk driver.

Not long after the bus enters the freeway, the driver loses control of the bus. It zigzags, hits one car, then another, and then smashes into a railing. The car drivers are lucky. They escape with minor injuries. Some of the boys are not so lucky. Five of them are dead even before paramedics can reach them. The bus driver escapes with a minor injury. He faces a jail term. But that is not the worst for him. All his life he will carry a burden. All his life he will see the faces of the boys whose lives he took. Death would have been an act of mercy.

A man goes to a party. He drinks beer. He drinks one can too many. The party is at a friend's house. The man could have stayed the night at the house. He could have waited until he was sober enough to drive. He could have asked someone sober to drive him home. But he was confident that he could drive. Six cans! I could drink more than that, he says to himself as he goes. He enters a one-way roadway and slams into an oncoming car. Death was merciful and took him. Death also took two innocent lives.

Mothers are mad (MADD — Mothers Against Drunk Drivers). They are mad at drunk drivers, and rightly so. Drunk drivers take away their husbands, sons, and daughters. Drunk drivers take away a beloved part of their lives. Drunk drivers leave a wound so deep that even time can hardly heal it.

Shouldn't we all get mad at drunk drivers? There should not only be a fad (FADD — Fathers Against Drunk Drivers) against drunk driving. There should be a permanent mutual defense system against these unguided missiles on the road. The best defense against the menace of drunk driving is keeping drunk drivers off the road. If you drink, don't drive. The life you save may be yours.

A MONSTER CALLED DRUGS

Len Bias was an awesome athlete. He had enormous talents. He had a bright future. Just out of college, he was joining the Boston Celtics. His passage to fame and fortune seemed sure and certain. Death intervened. Cocaine, a killer drug, took another victim.

Cocaine comes from the leaves of the coca plant. Coca grows wild in Peru and Bolivia. The danger of cocaine use is addiction. It can come within weeks of use. It is easy to get hooked on the drug. Like opium, it engenders euphoria, a feeling of well-being. It sharpens mental powers and makes fatigue disappear. The cocaine user does not feel hunger or thirst; the opium user is relieved of his pains. However, repeated use weakens both of these effects. The user must use more and more to get the desired result. Opium shortens life; cocaine can end it suddenly by respiratory failure, just as it did in the case of Len Bias.

Len Bias is not the only victim. There are many more like him. Some are as famous as he. Others are nameless persons — bums and drifters. Death for these people is an act of mercy, for the life of a drug addict is a living hell. Drug addiction, misery, and crime are sure companions. To support the drug habit, the user often resorts to a life of crime. That is not unusual. His addiction would have caused him to lose his job, if he had one. If he had none to begin with, he would not be able to find a job because of his addiction. The addict is depressed, suspicious, and easily irritated. His mental powers are diminished. Because of this, he is dangerous.

If this is not bad enough, hundreds of thousands of babies are born to addicted mothers. Some die. Some live, permanently impaired for life. Most of them are born prematurely. Cocaine use leads to early labor. How does cocaine affect the babies? No one really knows. What is known however, is that cocaine is very addictive. Monkeys in labs are observed to inject themselves with cocaine for days until they die. Yes, drugs are evil. They harm people in many, many ways. They reach into the womb and touch babies, too.

(Sources: "Cocaine," Vol. 5, and "Drugs," Vol. 7, *Encyclopedia Britannica*, 1973 ed.; *Discover*, Sep. '89.)

THE LITTERBUG, THE WORSE KIND OF BUG

There are many kinds of bugs. All bugs do a job in Nature. In that sense there are no bad bugs. Some bugs, like the bedbug and the assassin bug, however, bite humans and spread disease. Others like aphids, leaf hoppers, lice, and potato bugs harm our crops and plants. So we say they are bad. Other bugs eat other harmful bugs and so reduce their menace to us. Many, like the water boatmen, serve as food for animals. Still others are the source of waxes and dyes. These are the good bugs.

One bug that is curious and queer is the cicada. It stays some 20 feet deep under the ground for 17 years. When it comes out, the cicada makes a piercing, metallic noise. It is good that only the male has a "voice" and that cicadas live very briefly. If the cicada is an interesting but brief-living bug, there is one that lives long and is disgusting. It may be seen on roads and beaches and in parks, picnic areas, cinemas and other public areas. It comes in all sizes and makes all sorts of noises. What makes it a great peril is that it is found in almost any area in the world. You will even see signs of mental life and suspect it has intelligence. Perhaps, it really is intelligent; if so, it is thoughtless and without care.

The cicada leaves its old skin behind and flies out to find a mate. Then it dies. The litterbug leaves behind paper bags, beer cans, cups, cigars, butts, leftover food, diapers, tires, wires, bottles and caps, oil filters, air filters, hoses, metal bits, pieces of wood, and all kinds of refuse as it drives out to go back home. Then it goes out again to do the same thing. The litterbug makes our roads, beaches, picnic areas, parks and other public areas ugly and dirty. The problem is, we cannot squash it as we do a bedbug when the bedbug bites us, and unlike the cicada, it is a bug for all seasons.

GLOSSARY

abattoir — slaughterhouse

adage — old saying; a maxim

addax — a large antelope

agate — a very hard stone with patches of color

aghast — horrified

agile — fast

antique — an old thing which is rare

artesian well — a well which has been bored vertically on the ground so that water
  will rise to the surface with little or no pumping

assure — to make sure

auction — a public sale

audition — a hearing to test the ability of entertainers such as singers and musicians

awl — pointed tool for making holes in such materials as wood and leather

Bach — German composer

bale — a large bundle or package prepared for shipping, storage or sale

balk — to miss intentionally

beige — grayish-tan color

bilk — to cheat; to swindle

bobbin — the reel that holds the thread

Bordeaux — wine region in France

bouquet — a bunch of flowers

boutique — a small, retail, specialty shop

brawn — muscular strength

brine — water with salt

bronco — partly tamed horse

burr — a prickly seed envelope

bustle — to move or act with a great show of energy

buxom — healthy or comely; said of a woman or a girl

cachalot — the sperm whale

cafe — coffee house

casual — accidental, unplanned

caulk — to make water-tight

cell — a small room in a prison

censure — to blame

chaise — a lightweight horse-drawn carriage with a collapsible top

chaos — disorder

chassis — the main frame of a car, airplane, or truck

chauffeur — driver

chef — head cook

chemise — a woman's undergarment

chic — smart elegance

chiffon — a sheer silk cloth used for women's dresses

chlorine — a yellow-green poisonous gas

cholera — an intestinal disease; an infectious disease causing acute diarrhea

Chopin — a Polish composer

insure — to protect from damage

chameleon — a lizard that changes color to blend with its surroundings

chasm — abyss, gorge

chrism — holy oil used in baptism

chrome — chromium alloy used in plating

cinch — sure grip; a saddle or pack girth

cinder — a piece of burnt matter not yet reduced to ashes
clack — to make a quick, sharp sound; n. a sharp sound
cob — a male swan; a strong stocky horse
convey — to transport
composite — made of distinct parts; compound
conceptual — pertaining to the formation of general ideas
condemn — to blame
convoy — a protecting escort
corsage — a bouquet of flowers for a woman to wear
coupe — closed two door car that seats two to six persons
Cousteau — French undersea explorer; inventor of the aqualung
crawfish — the crayfish
crayfish — fresh-water crustacean, related to lobster
creel — a wicker basket for holding fish
crick — a painful cramp at the back of the neck
cruise — to travel from place to place for pleasure
crypt — vault under the main floor of a church used as a burial place
cuisine — art of preparing and cooking food
curfew - time of day or night when persons (all or specific categories)
   are not allowed in the streets
cygnet — a young swan
cyst — an abnormal sac formed in the body containing fluid or semisolid matter
dab — to apply quick, gentle pressure on any surface with something soft
dash — to rush
daze — to shock
debris — rubbish; ruins
debut — first public appearance of an actor; formal introduction of a girl to society
decoy — a lure
deem — consider
depot — a storehouse
din — noise
dome — roof with a half-rounded shape
dominion — the kingdom, realm or rule of a king
dose — an amount of medicine
doze — to sleep lightly
douse — to plunge into water
dread — great fear
dreary — cheerless, dull
drover — a cattle dealer
dub — to make a knight by touching the shoulder with a sword
dun — grayish-brown; v. to ask persistently for the payment of a debt
enthrall — to fascinate
era — a period in history
erode — to wear away
escritoire — a writing desk
etiquette — rules of correct behavior
eunuch — a castrated man who guards a harem
Eurasia — Europe and Asia taken as one
exempt — to free from a rule
exile — to force a person out of his country; the person himself
exotic — foreign; strangely beautiful
fad — a temporary fashiion or manner of conduct
fag — to tire out

fancy — imagination or inclination
feud — a bitter, continuous quarrel
fissure — a cleft made by separation of parts
flaw — a defect
fleece — wool covering a sheep
flounder — a flatfish; to struggle awkwardly
forefront; the first part or place
fraud — deceit
freak — an odd person or animal
freight — cargo
fringe — border
frisk — to search for a weapon
fuss — to worry about small things
futile — useless
gauze — loosely woven cloth
ghastly — horrible
ghoul — an evil spirit that feeds on the corpses
gibber — to make unintelligible sounds, specially when excited or afraid
gibbet — the gallows
giblet — the edible innards of birds
giddy — to have a feeling that everything is spinning around
gild — to coat with a thin layer of gold
gleam — a ray of light
glean — to gather information
glen — a secluded valley
glimmer — flickering, faint
gloom — to become dark; to be or look dejected
glum — sullen
glut — to flood the market with goods
glutton — a person who eats to excess
gnaw — to wear away bit by bit
gnu — a large antelope
goby — small spiny fish
grief — sadness
groggy — staggering, as from exhaustion or blows
grub — a short, fat worm
grudge — ill-will
gruff — rough in manner and speech
Guadalcanal — one of the Solomon Islands in the South Pacific
Guam — one of the Marianas Islands in the Pacific: a U.S. territory
guano — the manure of sea birds
guava — tropical tree bearing a yellowish pear shaped fruit used as preserves
guild — any group with a common interest
Guinevere — in legend, the wife of King Arthur
guppy — small tropical fish
hack — to cut by repeated strokes
hackle — slender feathers at the neck of a rooster
haze — light fog
heave — to throw a heavy thing
heed — to listen to
hellion — mischievous person
hoax — a trick
hock — middle joint of an animal's hind legs; v. to pawn

hull — the body of a ship; husk of a seed

imbecile — idiot

irate — angry

irrigate — to supply with water with the use of ditches

irritate — to annoy

isthmus — a strip of land with water on both sides connecting two large land masses

jade — a highly sought mineral stone, usually carved decoratively; to wear out

jag — a sharp projection

jib — a triangular sail

jig — a device for fishing; a lively dance

kayak — Eskimo canoe

keen — sharp

ken — knowledge

keno — a gambling game like lotto

kin — relatives

knave — deceitful man

knell — to ring in a mournful way

knick-knack — trinket

knoll — a mound; a little rounded hill

kola nut — seed of a West African tree used in making soft drinks (also spelled cola)

Korea — a country in eastern Asia, divided into North and South Korea

Kuwait — oil-rich Mideast country

lacquer — clear varnish

larceny — theft

leisure — ease; free time for rest and recreation

loiter — to spend time lazily

lop — to cut away branches and twigs

luscious — gratifying to the taste or smell

lug — to carry or drag with difficulty

lurch — to sway suddenly from side to side

luscious — delicious, sweet, and juicy

lynx — wild animal of the cat family

malice — ill-will; hatred

malicious — evil; wicked

matinee — afternoon show

medallion — a large medal

memoir — a biography

menace — threat, danger

mirage — optical illusion; anything that falsely appears real

moire — silk with a wavy pattern

Monet — French impressionist painter

mortgage — pledging of property to secure a debt

mosque — a Moslem place of worship

myrrh — fragrant resin exuded by shrubs of Arabia and East Africa used in making incense

nanny — a child's nurse

negate — to deny

neutral — not taking sides

nil — nothing

nominee — a person named for an honor or office

nook — a secluded place

nymph — in mythology, a semi-divine maiden living in the woods or sea

obnoxious — hateful; offensive

orate — to make a speech

oust — to throw out

parquet — wood tiles

passion — any strong feeling

peer — an equal; to look narrowly

perceptual — mental image derived from the senses

pestle — implement to grind grain in a mortar

philosopher — one who searches by logical reasoning for the basic truths and principles
  of life, for morals of the universe, and to discover how we understand and perceive things

phobia — a lasting, abnormal fear

phoenix — in legend, a bird that rose from its own ashes

piffle — anything nonsensical

pip — any of the small seeds of fruits such as apples, oranges and pears

plateau — an elevated tract of more or less level land

phlegm — mucus

pneumonia — inflammation of the tissues of the lungs

potpourri — mixture of dried petals with spices kept in a jar for its fragrance

prejudice — an opinion not based on fact; bias

prism — anything that bends light

prowess — superior ability, skill, or technique

prudent — cautious

Psalter — The Book of Psalms

psychotic — one having a mental disorder that leads to a seriously disorganized personality

psychopath — a person with a serious personality disorder

psychology — the science of the mind

pub — a tavern

quartz — a semiprecious stone

quaver — to vibrate

query — an inquiry

quota — a share

quote — to repeat

rap — a sharp, light blow

reel — to stagger; a revolving frame

rendezvous — a meeting; v. to meet

Renoir — French painter

repertoire — stock of plays, songs and dances that an actor, singer or company does

reservoir — an artificial or natural place where water is collected and stored

résumé — a summary

reverie — a state of dreamy meditation

rhubarb — a plant with large leaves used as food

richochet — to bounce off a surface

rogue — a vagabond; a scoundrel

rouge — various reddish cosmetic powders and pastes for coloring cheeks, lips

rowdy — a rough, riotous fellow

rudder — anything that guides a course

ruse — a trick

rut — deep track made by wheels on soft ground

schooner — a ship with two masts rigged fore and aft

science — systematic knowledge

scimitar — a short, broad sword with an edge on the convex side used by Turks and Arabs

scion — a descendant, an heir

scotch — to put down; to injure without killing, to maim

scow — large, flat bottomed boat used for carrying cargo

scrabble — to scribble; to scrape

scrawl — to write awkwardly
scribe — a writer
scribble — to write carelessly
scrod — a codfish prepared for cooking
scroll — a roll of parchment or paper with writing on it
scrounge — to seek out and gather
seer — a prophet
seraph — an angel of the highest order
shabby — beggarly, worn out
shrapnel — fragment of an exploded shell
shrew — small mouse-like animal
shrine — a place where holy things are kept
shroud — cloth to wrap the dead
skein — quantity of wool or yarn wound in a coil
skewer — metal or wooden pin to hold meat for cooking
slake — to make less intense, satisfy, as in to slake a thirst
sloop — a small sailing vessel with a mainsail and a jib
slouch — a lazy person
smelt — small trout-like fish; to separate impurities from a metal ore by melting
smew — a member of the duck family
smite — to punish; to affect suddenly
smudge — smear, stain
snicker — to laugh in a sly, stifled manner
sniffle — to sniff repeatedly, from a head cold or to repress emotion
snorkel — device with air intake and exhaust to allow breathing under water
sow — a female pig
spangle — small piece of bright metal
spawn — the mass of eggs emitted by a fish
splendid — brilliant
splendor — magnificence; glory
spleen — an organ near the upper left part of the abdomen
splotch — a stain
splurge — any extravagant display or effort
sprat — a small fish of the herring family
sprite — a fairy
sprocket — any of the teeth of a wheel arranged to fit a chain
squall — brief, violent windstorm
squander — spend wastefully
squash — to crush
squirm — to wriggle
sty — a pigpen; inflamed swelling on the edge of the eyelid
sullen — ill-tempered in a quiet way
surety — guarantor; certainty
survey — to determine area and boundary of land
swoon — to faint
teem — to be full of
teeter — to see-saw; to waver
thatch — roofing made of leaves and straws
thong — a narrow strip of leather
thresher — one who beats the husk from the grain
throng — a multitude gathered together
tipsy — slightly unsteady because of alcoholic drink
toddy — sweetened drink of liquor and hot water
toupee- a wig; hair piece

trawl — a large net dragged along the bottom of the sea for fishing
treacle — molasses
trowel — a garden implement
truce — temporary stop to fighting
tun — a large cask for beer or wine
tumor — abnormal mass of tissue growing on or in the body
twaddle — foolish talk or writing
twang — sharp, nasal speech
twiddle — to play with; a twirling motion
undertow — current below the surface of the water
vandal — destroyer of property
vane — weather cock
veal — meat of the calf
venom — poison
vex — to annoy
vim — force; energy
viper — a poisonous snake
vulgar — unrefined; in bad taste
wad — a roll of money; a small, soft mass
weasel — a sneaky person
wharf — a pier, a place for boats to dock
whet — to sharpen
whopper — anything that is large
whoop — a loud cry; the hoot of the owl
wobble — to move from side to side unsteadily
wonder — to marvel
wraith — an apparition, a ghost
wrasse — a spiny, brightly colored fish
xebec — a three masted ship that once sailed the Mediterranean
xenon — a gaseous chemical element
xerus — any of the African ground squirrels
xylem — woody part of a plant that conducts moisture
yacht — a pleasure boat
yawl — a small sailboat
yen — intense desire; Japanese coin
yodel — to sing with abrupt change from normal chest sounds to falsetto
yoga — a philosophy of physical and mental discipline
   to attain a union with the supreme being
yonder — over there, farther
yucca — plant of the lily family
zax — a tool for cutting slate
zebu — ox-like domestic animal in Asia and Africa with a large hump and short curving horns
Zeppelin — large, rigid, cigar shape dirigible balloon
zodiac — imaginary belt of the heavens, including 12 constellations
   which astrologers use to predict the future
zombie — in West Indian lore, a corpse in trance-like animation

REFERENCES:

Chall, Jeanne S. *Learning to Read: The Great Debate*. New York: McGraw-Hill, New York, 1967.

Mazurkiewicz, Albert J. *Teaching About Phonics*. New York: St. Martin's Press, 1976.

Flesch, Rudolph. *Why Johnny Can't Read and What You Can Do About It*. New York: Harper and Brothers, 1955.

Why Johnny Still Can't Read. New York: Harper and Row, 1981.

Parker, Robert P. and Frances A. David, eds. *Developing Literacy: Young Children's Use of Language*. Newark: International Reading Association, 1983.

Harris, Albert J. *How to Increase Reading Ability*, 5th ed., Revised and Enlarged. New York: David McKay, 1970.

Heilmann, Arthur W., Timothy R. Blair and William H. Ruply. *Principles and Practices of Teaching Reading*, 6th ed. Columbus OH: Charles E. Merrill, 1986.

Morrow, Lesley M. *Literacy Development in the Early Years, Helping Children Read and Write*. Engelwood Cliffs NJ: Prentice Hall, 1989.

Hymes, James L., Jr. *Teaching the Child Under Six*, 3rd. ed. Columbus OH: Charles Merrill, 1981.

Forgan, Harry W. *Help Your Child Learn to Read; New Ways To Make Learning Fun*. Toronto: Pagurian Press, 1975.

Wilson, Robert M. and and Mary Anne Hall. *Programmed Word Attack for Teachers*, 4th ed. Columbus OH: Charles E. Merrill, 4th edition.

Kidd, J. R.. *How Adults Learn*. New York: Associated Press, 1976.

Johnson, Barbara. *Helping your Child Achieve in School*. Novato CA: Arena Press, 1985.

Gettman, David. *Basic Montessori*. New York: St. Martin's Press, 1987.

Martin, John Henry and Ardy Friedberg. *Writing to Read*. New York: Warner Books, 1986.

Montessori, Maria. *Dr. Montessori's Own Handbook*. Cambridge MA: Robert Bentley, 1966.

Bond, Guy L. and Miles A. Tinker. *Reading Difficulties: Their Diagnosis and Correction*. Engelwood Cliffs NJ: Prentice Hall, 1973.

Bolles Blair, Edmund E. *Remembering and Forgetting: Inquiries into the Nature of Memory*. New York: Walker Publishing, 1988.

Blumenfeld, Samuel. *The New Illiterates And How You Can Keep Your Child from Becoming One*. New Rochelle NY: Arlington House, 1973.

The Winston Dictionary, Advanced Edition. Atlanta GA: John C. Winston, 1951.

Erhlich, Eugene et. al. *Oxford American Dictionary*. New York: Oxford University Press, 1980.

Guralnik, David B., General Editor. *Webster's New World Dictionary of the American Language*. Nashville TN: Southwestern, 1964.

Encyclopedia Britannica. Chicago: William Benton, 1973.

Albrecht, Karl. *Brain Power*. Englewood Cliffs NJ: Prentice-Hall, 1980.

Lewis, David and James Greene. *Thinking Better*. New York: Rawson, Wade Publishers, 1982.

Additional copies of
E-Z Reader: Learning to Read the Phonics Way
by Perfecto G. Querubin, Jr., may be ordered by
sending a check or money order
for $17.95 postpaid for each copy to:

DISTINCTIVE PUBLISHING CORP.
P.O. Box 17868
Plantation FL 33318-7868
(305) 975-2413

Quantity discounts are also available
from the publisher